Traveling Together

Books by

Karla Worley

From New Hope Publishers

Glimpses of Christ in Everyday Lives

Growing Weary Doing Good?

When the Glass Slipper Doesn't Fit (with Claire Cloninger)

Traveling Together

Thoughts on Women, Friendship,

and the Journey of Faith

Karla Worley

New Hope Publishers

Birmingham, Alabama

New Hope® Publishers
P. O. Box 12065
Birmingham, AL 35202-2065
www.newhopepubl.com

Library of Congress Cataloging-in-Publication Data
Worley, Karla.
Traveling together : thoughts on women, friendship, and the journey of faith /
Karla Worley.
    p. cm.
ISBN 1-56309-721-4 (pbk.)
1. Christian women—Religious life. 2. Female friendship-Religious aspects—
Christianity. I. Title.
BV4527 .W635 2003
241'.6762'082—dc21
2002013012

All Scripture quotations, unless otherwise indicated, are taken from the HOLY
BIBLE, NEW INTERNATIONAL VERSION®. NIV®. Copyright ©1973, 1978,
1984 by International Bible Society. Used by permission of Zondervan. All rights
reserved.

Scripture quotations marked (NASB) are taken from the NEW AMERICAN
STANDARD BIBLE®, Copyright © 1960, 1962, 1963, 1968, 1971, 1972, 1973,
1975, 1977, 1995 by The Lockman Foundation. Used by permission.

Scripture quotations marked (*The Message*) are taken from *The Message* by Eugene
H. Peterson, Copyright (c) 1993, 1994, 1995, 1996, 2000. Used by permission of
NavPress Publishing Group. All rights reserved.

Scripture quotations marked (AMP) are taken from the Amplified Bible,
Copyright © 1954, 1958, 1962, 1964, 1965, 1987 by The Lockman Foundation.
Used by permission.

Any emphasis in italics is added by the author.

Cover design by Cheryl Totty

Cover photo © Digital Vision

ISBN: 1-56309-721-4

N024117 • 0203 • 5M1

For Saralu

tender, wise, funny, flaky, faithful, firecracker.

Thank you for more than twenty years

of traveling together on the journey of faith.

I love you, dear friend.

Table of Contents

Acknowledgments

This was a difficult book to write. Partly because I knew my friends would read it, and having been my friends for a while now, they know that I do not understand or live everything in this book. I am—we all are—still learning how to be a friend. It is a lifelong process.

Picasso said that an artist paints not to ask a question, but because he has found something, and he wants to share—he cannot help it—what he has found. I have come late in life to find the sustaining power of friendship with women. That's because I didn't allow myself the opportunity before. I was too busy, or too busy pretending to be strong, to know the joy and gratitude that comes with admitting the pure human need for company. I am so grateful that God caused me to be weak so that I would have to lean. That is how I discovered so many of the things I want to tell you about friendship and women and faith. I learned how to be a friend from these women who are my friends.

I wish I could introduce you to each other. I would want you to meet Kim and Vicki. I would want you to meet Saralu. I'd love for you to meet Sheryl and Mollie and many other women friends who faithfully and boldly live their journey of faith in countries around the world. I wish you could know the women who have wrestled for me in prayer during some very personal battles—Laura, Monica,

Janet, Barbara, Cindy, Debbie, Esther, and the other Barbara. I'd introduce you to Susan and Kellie and my neighbor, Amy. Where would I be without these women? And where would you be without the women who are your friends in the faith? That's what I hope you come to find in these pages.

These pages would not be here without the encouragement and skill of my editor, Leslie Caldwell. I thank you, Leslie, for your patience and your trust in me. Thank you for adopting each book as your very own. Thank you for your steady competence. I thank all of the very special people at New Hope Publishers who said "Yes" to the idea of this book and gave it a home and a future.

I am grateful to Dr. Gene Getz for his book *The Walk: Growing into the Fullness of Christ*, which made the New Testament model of walking worthy together come alive for me. Two other books inspired and influenced my understanding of the Christian life in community: Eugene Peterson's *The Wisdom of Each Other: A Conversation Between Spiritual Friends* and Dietrich Bonhoeffer's *Life Together*. I also learned a great deal from *I Know Just What You Mean: The Power of Friendship in Women's Lives* by Ellen Goodman and Patricia O'Brien. You should read all of these books!

Finally, I thank four very special guys: Dennis, Seth, Matt, and Ben Worley, who did their own laundry, made their own dinners, and put up with a wife and mother who had not slept or combed her hair in weeks. I could write a whole book about how much I love you.

Karla Worley
Franklin, Tennessee
2002

Introduction
Traveling Together

You were all called to travel on the same road and in the same direction, so stay together, both outwardly and inwardly.
—Ephesians 4:3 The Message

The ferry to Shen Zhen pulled away just before sunset. We sat by the wide window, craning our necks as we watched mainland China recede from view. We had made it, finally made it, on this journey so anticipated.

Just six months earlier it had been canceled in the wake of the terrorists' attack on the US on September 11, 2001. Now our adventure was almost completed. I watched through tears. This trip had been a dream come true. When I was a little girl I read the story of the missionary Lottie Moon. Since then, I had wanted to see China. And here I was, saying good-bye to it.

I turned to my traveling companion—my dear friend, my sister-in-law, Kim, who sat beside me.

"We did it," I said.

We began planning this trip more than two years ago. For me, the journey was both a spiritual pilgrimage and a very real physical challenge. We had planned a rigorous itinerary, including some serious mountain climbing. My doctor had warned, "You will not go if your health doesn't improve." I had spent the past year dieting, disciplining, weight training. I had practically walked the equivalent of the distance to China and back! And my personal trainer, my encourager, my Coach Pain in the Rear had been my friend Kim.

"I wouldn't be here now if it wasn't for you," I whispered to her.

For Kim, the journey began more than ten years ago, when we first got to know each other. At that time, Kim was not a Christian. She knew almost nothing about God. Her new sister-in-law, the Bible teacher and *professional* Christian, was strange. Kim asked many questions. She watched and she listened. I walked with her on her way to know God and prayed with her on the day that she invited Jesus Christ to change her life. At times I have been her own spiritual Coach Pain in the Rear. And when I shared my childhood dream to visit China, Kim said, "I'm going, too."

Now she looked at me with tears in her own eyes and whispered back, "If it wasn't for you, I wouldn't be here, either."

Traveling together, we had made the journey.

"It is not good for man to be alone," God observed at creation, thereafter fashioning a companion. We were made to live in community—in community with God and with others. In the Old Testament, God's covenants with individuals are made for the purpose of establishing, protecting, or providing for a community. God's prophecies are given to a community. His judgments are pronounced against a community, His mercy extended to a community.

When Jesus came, He "came to His own" (John 1:11 NASB), plural—a community. Jesus lived in community. He called and empowered a community. He commissioned a community. This was His vision for us—"that all of them may be one, Father, just as you are in me and I am in you" (John 17:21).

God Himself is a community—Father, Son, and Holy Spirit, three in one. We, called to be like Him, are called into that mysterious many-becoming-one relationship. It is part of the process of becoming more like Him, this relinquishing of our individual rights and concerns, tossing them into the collective stream of discipleship and service called the Body of Christ.

The apostle Paul understood this when he wrote to

the New Testament churches about their spiritual growth, their disciplines, their attitudes. His letters, recorded in Greek, were written, for the most part, in the plural person. When Paul said, "I urge you," he was not talking to me; he was talking to me and you. Together we grow. Together we co-labor. Together we persevere. Together we endure. Together we inherit, enjoy, rejoice.

"I urge you to live a life worthy of the calling you have received," Paul wrote to the community of believers in Ephesians 4:1, and he went on to describe this Christlike communal life: "Be completely humble and gentle; be patient, bearing with one another in love. Make every effort to keep the unity of the Spirit through the bond of peace" (Eph. 4: 2–3).

What is the basis for the lifestyle Paul prescribed? "There is one body and one Spirit—just as you were called to one hope when you were called—one Lord, one faith, one baptism; one God and Father of all, who is over *all* and through *all* and in *all*" (Eph. 4:4–6).

Yes, within the "all" of community, God does get personal. Paul went on to explain how and why God works through individuals in this community. "But to each one of us grace has been given as Christ apportioned it. This is why it says: 'When he ascended on high, he led captives in his train and gave gifts to men.' (What does 'he ascended' mean except that he also descended to the lower, earthly regions? He who descended is the very one who ascended higher than all the heavens, in order to fill the whole universe.) It was he who gave some to be apostles, some to be prophets, some to be evangelists, and some to be pastors and teachers" (Eph. 4:7–11).

God Himself became an individual when He "descended to the lower earthly regions." Why? "In order to fill the whole universe." When God gets personal, it is to engage an individual in His agenda for the community. God became personal with Abraham in order to birth the Hebrew nation. God became personal with Moses in order to deliver the Israelites from Egypt. God became personal with Isaiah in order to speak to the nation of Judah. He became personal with Jeremiah in order to speak to the nation of Israel. He became personal with Paul in order to reach beyond the Jews to engage the rest of humanity. God draws us to Himself individually, saves us individually, gifts us individually—but not so that each may be a single perfect specimen of holiness. Rather, it is: "To prepare God's people for works of service, so that the body of Christ may be built up until *we all* reach unity in the faith and in the knowledge of the Son of God and become mature, attaining to the whole measure of the fullness of Christ" (Eph. 4:12–13).

It is not enough that I become Christlike, nor that you become Christlike. The "whole measure" is not reached until "the whole body, joined and held together by every supporting ligament, grows and builds itself up in love, as each part does its work" (Eph. 4:16).

In the late twentieth century, particularly in the

United States, culture became me-centered. Emphasis was on personal achievement, personal profit, personal rights and ambitions, sometimes to the point of sacrificing the common good. That cultural mind-set has permeated the church as we have become spiritual consumers. Does this get *me* closer to God? Does this make *me* more holy? Does this contribute to *my* spiritual growth? Does it make *me* wiser, healthier, happier, more successful? We have begun to interpret the Bible's teachings in first personal singular: I, me, mine.

"Our society practically worships privacy," writes author Ann Hibbard in *Treasured Friends*. "We unwittingly embrace the philosophy of 'What I do is my business, and what you do is your business.'" This is the doctrine of relativism; it is the prevalent philosophy of our day. Truth is relative; values depend upon circumstances. In a relativistic society, there is no absolute truth, nor is there an absolute authority. I have no right to tell you how you should live, nor should you presume to tell me. A believer must understand this philosophy. I must recognize that when I submit to God as the absolute authority and to His Word as absolute truth, I am living in direct opposition to my culture. I am swimming upstream. This can be a lonely way of life. That's why one believer needs another believer. It's an individual choice to recognize and follow Christ. To those who are willing to walk by faith, God gives the gift of community, of companionship on the way.

When Jesus came to the region of Caesarea Philippi, he asked his disciples, "Who do people say the Son of Man is?"

They replied, "Some say John the Baptist; others say Elijah; and still others, Jeremiah or one of the prophets."

"But what about you?" he asked. "Who do you say I am?"

Simon Peter answered, "You are the Christ, the Son of the living God."

Jesus replied, "Blessed are you, Simon son of Jonah, for this was not revealed to you by man, but by my Father in heaven. And I tell you that you are Peter, and *on this rock I will build my church*, and the gates of Hades will not overcome it. I will give you the keys of the kingdom of heaven; whatever you bind on earth will be bound in heaven, and whatever you loose on earth will be loosed in heaven."

—Matthew 16:13–19

Peter alone recognized the truth when he saw it. Peter alone saw by faith and responded by faith. Upon this one person's confession, Jesus established a community—the church, the body of believers who by faith recognize and obey Christ. He appointed that community to do His will on earth. He authorized that community by imparting to them a power that had the weight of heaven thrown behind it: "I will give you the keys of the kingdom of heaven; whatever you bind on earth will be bound in heaven, and whatever you loose on earth will be loosed in heaven" (Matt. 16:19).

In *The Body*, Charles Colson writes, "The church was to be His instrument on earth, and whatever was done in His will would have eternal significance and consequence." Jesus did not give this appointment and authority to Peter. He gave it to the church. Not to an individual but to a community.

"Again, I tell you that if *two of you on earth* agree about anything you ask for, it will be done for you by my Father in heaven. For where *two or three come together in my name*, there am I with them" (Matt. 18:18–20). Here is an explosive truth. Read that passage again carefully. A community of faith may be a congregation of 3,000 members or an entire denomination. The community of faith may mean the universal body of believers, or it may mean a handful of disciples who meet secretly in a house somewhere under a communist regime. The "keys of the kingdom," the power to bind or loose as if Christ Himself were doing it, is given where *just two* gather in His name. The appointment and authority is bestowed even upon two friends meeting over a cup of coffee! If we are believers, our friendship is a church.

This can be true because Christ configured the church not as a building, but as a people. The Greek word *ekklesia*, translated in the New Testament as "church," does not refer to a structure but a group of people. "Nowhere in the New Testament does anyone say, 'Let's go to church,' nor is the church referred to as a building, except as a metaphor. All references to the church, including the metaphorical 'body' and 'holy nation,' refer to God's people, built on the foundation of the apostles and prophets, with Christ Jesus Himself as the chief cornerstone," writes Charles Colson in *The Body*. "In him the whole building is joined together and rises to become a holy temple in the Lord," Paul wrote. "And in him you too are being built *together* to become a dwelling in which God lives by his Spirit" (Eph. 2:21–22).

The apostle Peter wrote: "You also, like living stones, are being built into a spiritual house to be a holy priesthood . . . you are a chosen people, a royal priesthood, a holy nation, a people belonging to God, that you may declare the praises of him who called you out of darkness into his wonderful light. Once you were not a people, but now you are the people of God; once you had not received mercy, but now you have received mercy" (1 Peter 2:5, 9–10).

If the church is a people, it is not just any people, Peter says. *Ekklesia* is derived from the Greek verb *kaleo* (to call) and the Greek preposition *ek* (out of). We are "the called out ones." We are called out from the culture into a covenant relationship with God. We are called out for a purpose. We are called out to be commissioned, and we are commissioned together: a holy nation. The word *holy* means "set apart," or literally, "other." The church is not just a community, it is a new community, an altogether *other* community. It is a counterculture.

Nowhere is this seen more clearly than in the community of believers found in Jerusalem just following the events of the Passover week, Christ's ascension, and Pentecost:

> **They devoted themselves to the apostles' teaching and to the fellowship, to the breaking of bread and to prayer. Everyone was filled with awe, and many wonders and miraculous signs were done by the apostles. All the believers were together and had everything in common. Selling their possessions and goods, they gave to anyone as he had need. Every day they continued to meet together in the temple courts. They broke bread in their homes and ate together with glad and sincere hearts, praising God and enjoying the favor of all the people. And the Lord added to their number daily those who were being saved. —Acts 2:42–47**

The city of Jerusalem would have been jammed with Jews who had made the pilgrimage for the annual Passover feast, remaining after the astounding events of

Christ's arrest, death, and rumored resurrection. Camped out in every inn, house, and street, the pilgrims had come for just a week; now they were running out of food and money. With those in need, the small band of believers shared what few possessions they had. They performed miracles. They faithfully gathered in the temple courts to pray, offer sacrifices, and debate the Scriptures. In between, they ate together, laughed, told stories, and sang songs as friends do. The temple leaders and tourists all watched this controversial little community—their comings and goings, their daily acts of generosity, faithfulness, and friendship. And they were charmed by it. They were drawn to it. And the Lord added to the believers' numbers *daily*.

Peter called this kind of community "a priesthood." Nation, priesthood—both are communities. But the distinction is important. Whereas *nation* focuses on citizenship, *priesthood* connotes function. The work of a priest is to go between people and God. Because we are a holy nation, believers belong to God. Because we are a royal priesthood, we connect others to God.

The apostle Paul understood this priestly role and applied it to his friendships. Although itinerant, Paul had deep and abiding friendships—not only with his traveling companions, Barnabas, John Mark, Timothy, Luke, and Silas, but also with the people who made up the churches Paul founded. When Paul planted a church, he sometimes spent years in one place. He lived and worked and ate among the people. He came to know them through long hours of conversation. He heard their fears and their confessions. He knew their families. He wrestled with them over the personal cost of following Christ. And when Paul left, he was constantly concerned for his friends' spiritual and physical welfare. He missed their company.

> We loved you so much that we were delighted to share with you not only the gospel of God but our lives as well, because you had become so dear to us. —1 Thessalonians 2:8

> God, whom I serve with my whole heart in preaching the gospel of his Son, is my witness how constantly I remember you in my prayers at all times; and I pray that now at last by God's will the way may be opened for me to come to you. —Romans 1:9–10

> God can testify how I long for all of you with the affection of Christ Jesus. . . . I hope in the Lord Jesus to send Timothy to you soon, that I also may be cheered when I receive news about you. —Philippians 1:8, 2:19

> But, brothers, when we were torn away from you for a short time (in person, not in

> thought), out of our intense longing we
> made every effort to see you. For we wanted
> to come to you—certainly I, Paul, did, again
> and again—but Satan stopped us. For what
> is our hope, our joy, or the crown in which
> we will glory in the presence of our Lord
> Jesus when he comes? Is it not you? Indeed,
> you are our glory and joy.
> —1 Thessalonians 2:17–20

Paul was also candid about his own needs and asked for help and support. This leader, so strong in the faith, openly acknowledged his need for his friends.

> We do not want you to be uninformed,
> brothers, about the hardships we suffered in
> the province of Asia. We were under great
> pressure, far beyond our ability to endure,
> so that we despaired even of life. Indeed, in
> our hearts we felt the sentence of death. But
> this happened that we might not rely on our-
> selves but on God, who raises the dead. He
> has delivered us from such a deadly peril,
> and he will deliver us. On him we have set
> our hope that he will continue to deliver us,
> as you help us by your prayers. Then many
> will give thanks on our behalf for the gra-
> cious favor granted us in answer to the

prayers of many. —2 Corinthians 1:8–11

As you know, it was because of an illness that I first preached the gospel to you. Even though my illness was a trial to you, you did not treat me with contempt or scorn. Instead, you welcomed me as if I were an angel of God, as if I were Christ Jesus himself. —Galatians 4:13–14

Do your best to come to me quickly, for Demas, because he loved this world, has deserted me and has gone to Thessalonica. Crescens has gone to Galatia, and Titus to Dalmatia. Only Luke is with me. Get Mark and bring him with you, because he is helpful to me in my ministry. I sent Tychicus to Ephesus. When you come, bring the cloak that I left with Carpus at Troas, and my scrolls, especially the parchments. . . . Do your best to get here before winter.
—2 Timothy 4:9–12, 21

Paul requested and relied on his friends' prayers.

Pray also for me, that whenever I open my mouth, words may be given me so that I will fearlessly make known the mystery of the gospel, for which I am an ambassador in chains. Pray that I may declare it fearlessly, as I should. —Ephesians 6:19–20

Brothers, pray for us. —1 Thessalonians 5:25

Finally, brothers, pray for us that the message of the Lord may spread rapidly and be honored, just as it was with you. And pray that we may be delivered from wicked and evil men, for not everyone has faith.
—2 Thessalonians 3:1–2

I particularly love the intimacy revealed in this practical request to his friends Philemon, Apphia, and Archippus:

And one thing more: Prepare a guest room for me, because I hope to be restored to you in answer to your prayers. —Philemon 1:22

Such passionate friendships might be considered a luxury for a person like Paul. Consider that he wrote to many of these friends by hand; I barely have time to return e-mails! Sandwiched between the burden of work, family obligation, and personal disciplines, friendship often becomes optional. Weighed against the added duties of ministry, personal prayer, and study, friendship can even seem frivolous—unless I understand, as Paul did, that what Jesus said is true: "Wherever two or three are gathered in My name, there I am with them." If we are believers, our friendship is a church. And I am your priest.

Paul was gripped by this powerful vision of priestly friendship. He understood that his role in his friends' lives was to connect them to God. Paul's goal in friendship was that he might encourage and further his friends in their walk with Christ.

> **For this reason, since the day we heard about you, we have not stopped praying for you and asking God to fill you with the knowledge of his will through all spiritual wisdom and understanding. And we pray this *in order that you may live a life worthy of the Lord* and may please him in every way: bearing fruit in every good work, growing in the knowledge of God.** —Colossians 1:9–10

> **We proclaim him, admonishing and teaching everyone with all wisdom, *so that we may present everyone perfect in Christ. To this end I labor,* struggling with all his energy, which so powerfully works in me.**
> —Colossians 1:28–29

I want you to know how much I am strug-gling for you **and for those at Laodicea, and for all who have not met me personally. My purpose is that they may be encouraged in heart and united in love, so that they may have the full riches of complete understand-ing, in order that they may know the mys-tery of God, namely, Christ, in whom are hidden all the treasures of wisdom and knowledge.** —Colossians 2:1–3

Listen to the language Paul used—words like *strug-gling* and *labor*. Paul was not just laboring on behalf of a church; he was laboring on behalf of his friends, because his friends *were* the church. If Paul's friends grew spiritu-ally, the church grew spiritually. If his friends became ma-ture in Christ, the church became mature in Christ. Paul's letters were written to a community of friends who had committed themselves to walk together toward a common destination: to follow in the footsteps of Christ, becoming more and more like Him along the journey.

In his letter to his friends in Ephesus, Paul challenged them to walk together "in a manner worthy" of this goal. "Do not walk as the Gentiles walk," Paul warned (Eph. 4:17). He called his friends in Corinth to account for the same thing: "Aren't you walking as mere humans?" (1 Cor. 3:3).

Two believers will not walk together in friendship in

the same way that two non-believers will walk together in friendship. "Mere humans" are self-serving: I will be good to you as long as you are good to me. Mere humans are self-motivated: I will be your friend when I feel like it. Mere humans are self-aggrandizing: I will be your friend if it helps me succeed. Mere humans are self-indulgent: I will be your friend if it makes me happy and is convenient. We share the same hobby or the same habit. We have similar tastes or life circumstances. As long as these remain in common, we stay friends.

Paul wrote to his friends in Ephesus that it was time to put off the old mere human self. It was time to understand their calling and their goal, so that they could properly function together. So you and I must understand our role in our believing friend's life, with its corresponding calling, goal, and function.

The calling upon our friendship is that we both become like Christ, that our friendship itself grows more like Christ as years and life events go by. Yes, each of us is called to be conformed to Him, but it is even more important that as a unit we gradually acquire and exhibit the characteristics of Christ, who is in all and through all. "This is a mystery," Paul said, speaking of the church. It is a mysterious process how God takes individuals and molds them together into one image, that of His Son. But He does it for a reason: "[The purpose is] that through the church the complicated, many-sided wisdom of God in all its infinite variety and innumerable aspects might now be made known to the angelic rulers and authorities (principalities and powers) in the heavenly sphere" (Eph. 3:10 AMP).

Our friendship is a model of the kingdom, a living demonstration. The Word becomes flesh. Our friendship is the chalkboard upon which God explains Himself, not only to those around us, but also to angels and those with power in heavenly places!

The goal of our friendship is that we both grow into fully mature "little Christs," which is the meaning of the word *Christian*. "Let us grow up in every way and in all things into Him, Who is the Head, [even] Christ, the Messiah, the Anointed One. For because of Him the whole body (the church, in all its various parts closely) joined and firmly knit together by the joints and ligaments with which it is supplied, when each part [with power adapted to its need] is working properly (in all its functions), grows to full maturity" (Eph. 4:15–16 AMP).

As we travel together toward our goal of full maturity, we are joined at the hip. One slows down for the other, carries the other, encourages the other, depends on the other. Each challenges, paces, corrects, spurs the other toward the goal. This goal determines our activities and behaviors, our priorities and function in each other's lives.

My function as your friend in Christ is to equip you to walk toward the goal. The question I must ask is: As your friend, how can I help you become more like Christ? In everything we do together—play, work, endure, enjoy, hope, plan, dream, celebrate—in every moment of our friendship, this is my role. The marvelous mystery and power of Jesus Christ is that because He is supreme over everything (Col. 1:18), He is able to use everything—including play, work, plans, dreams, endurance, and victory—to conform us to His image. Two Christian women who are friends do not do only *Christian things* together, but because they belong to Christ, everything they do together can be used by Christ for His purposes.

How important is a friendship between two women to the whole Body of believers? Can one friendship make a difference in one congregation? Yes. Take, for instance, Euodia and Syntyche. Their dysfunctional friendship was so disruptive that Paul singled them out in his letter to the Philippians. Addressing the church on how to live together as the Body of Christ, Paul stopped and made it a point to correct these two women. "I plead with Euodia and I plead with Syntyche to agree with each other in the Lord" (Phil. 4:2).

How embarrassing is that? It reminds me of my childhood, when my father, who was a minister of music, would pause while introducing a hymn and say (from the pulpit), "We will sing hymn number 453—as soon as my daughter in the third row turns around and stops talking!"

To make matters worse, Paul asked the *whole congregation* to assist these women in getting their act together: "Yes, and I ask you, loyal yokefellow, help these women who have contended at my side in the cause of the gospel, along with Clement and the rest of my fellow workers, whose names are in the book of life" (Phil. 4:3).

What made Paul think suddenly of Euodia and Syntyche? Their friendship was a perfect example of the problem Paul had just been addressing. "For, as I have often told you before and now say again even with tears, many live as enemies of the cross of Christ. Their destiny is destruction, their god is their stomach, and their glory is in their shame. Their mind is on earthly things. But our citizenship is in heaven. And we eagerly await a Savior from there, the Lord Jesus Christ, who, by the power that enables him to bring everything under his control, will transform our lowly bodies so that they will be like his glorious body" (Phil. 3:18–21).

In refusing to come to agreement, Euodia and Syntyche were living as "mere humans," not as those called after Christ. What each obviously wanted was not Christ's way, but her own way. These two friends had forgotten the calling and the goal. They had reduced their friendship to a universe of two. Meanwhile, Paul was trying to get his friends to see that they were engaged in the business of eternity.

Yes, the call, the goal, the function of the Body of Christ is accomplished when it is lived out between two women in the context of friendship. We are—friends, parents, children, employers, women—the stones with which Christ builds His church. Paul makes it clear: a unified focus on the goal, toward the goal, achieving the goal, is necessary. It is no less crucial for two women than for a pastor and his congregation. We are equally called to a worthy walk. You and I may travel together as friends. Others may walk together as family, in business, in ministry. But all must walk worthy or the Body will limp along—or worse, fail to finish the course.

"Whatever happens, conduct yourselves in a manner worthy of the gospel of Christ," Paul wrote his friends. "Then, whether I come and see you or only hear about you in my absence, I will know that you stand firm in one spirit, contending as one man for the faith of the gospel" (Phil. 1:27). "Contending as one" is a bit like running a three-legged sack race. I remember those races from Field Days in grade school. I remember being paired up, remember the rasp of the rough burlap sack, the frustration that my success depended upon the strength and determination of my partner. And I remember skinning my knee as we fell together, though I was sure it was not my fault.

Believers, like it or not, are in this race together. Sometimes we run in perfect rhythm. Sometimes we are the weaker partner. And sometimes we fall, even when it is not our fault. But if I run my own race, leaving you holding the bag, so to speak, the course will not be finished. Alone, we cannot attain to the *whole* measure of the fullness of Christ. Alone, we do not effect God's purpose for us in the world—"brought to complete unity to let the world know that you sent me and have loved them even as you have loved me" (John 17:23). Alone, we will not fulfill our destiny in Christ: "Then I heard what sounded like a great multitude, like the roar of rushing waters and like loud peals of thunder, shouting: 'Hallelujah! For our Lord God Almighty reigns. Let us rejoice and be glad and give him glory! For the wedding of the Lamb has come, and his bride has made herself ready. Fine linen, bright and clean, was given her to wear'" (Rev. 19:6–8).

At the end of time, when God's purposes are fulfilled, I alone will not stand before Him dressed as a bride. You alone will not stand before Him dressed as a bride. The wedding ceremony pictured is not Jesus and His millions of brides. The bride is us—all of us, together. The garments we are dressed in are the righteous acts (plural), or fine linen, of the saints (plural). Until you are ready and I am ready—until we are all ready—the bride has not made herself ready!

That is why as we "walk worthy of the calling we have received," we must travel together. Bearing each other's burdens. Strengthening those whose knees are weak. Praying for each other and with each other. Breaking bread together. Praising God together. Laboring together. Only by walking in step with Christ and each other will we walk worthy of our calling to become like Him.

This will be accomplished in a hundred little daily acts of friendship, in the phone calls, e-mails, cups of coffee. It will be demonstrated in the casseroles we bake, the hours we sit by the bedside, the guarantee that I will always take your children and you will always take my call. It will be worked out in the hard times, the failures, the moments of truth, when we celebrate each other's victories and when we spur each other on to the next step of faith.

My proposition is simple: Why not learn how to be better friends? Since we're all called to the same journey, why not travel together? Are you interested? *Well, where do we start?* you might ask. Good question. Jesus' disciples asked the same thing: "Show us the way." To which He replied, "I am the way."

So we must begin with Jesus, who is both "where we are" and "how to get there." We must look at Him and see where He leads us.

Walk with me, girlfriend.

Chapter One
I Call You Friends

Whoever claims to live in him
must walk as Jesus did.
—1 John 2:6

She was everything I was not, but wanted to be: Jackie Kennedy-like, with brown hair and luminous brown eyes. She was the popular one; I was the new girl with frizzy blonde hair and recently-acquired glasses. Yet miraculously, she was my best friend.

Together we did what fifth-grade girls did in the late sixties: passed notes in class, rode banana-seated bikes, endlessly debated who was the cutest of The Monkees (Davy Jones!), begged our mothers to let us shave our legs. And we pledged our undying friendship. We gave ourselves nicknames; she was Ginger, I was Honey. We had those names engraved on friendship rings, which turned our fingers green. Under the tree that was our clubhouse, we held a solemn ceremony in which we pricked our fingers and pressed them together, declaring ourselves blood sisters forever.

The adult world has no ceremony for initiating a friendship. We have wedding ceremonies, birthday traditions, baby dedications, even rituals for signing treaties, yet the contract of friendship has no solemn ritual.

But there is a ceremony of friendship within the Body of Christ: communion. In standard English usage, communion is defined as an intimate connection or relationship. In the Christian tradition, communion is that sacrament which celebrates the miracle of God becoming one in heart and flesh with the community of faith. It is the context in which Jesus announced a new relationship between God and man: "I call you friends." No longer would man be given a set of commandments, a list of expectations handed down by God's prophets. Now we would be drawn to God's side, to know His heart and share His secrets.

Christians are distinguished from all other disciples in that we have a God who comes to us, who chooses us, who draws us close even though it costs Him a terrible price. God chose a relationship with Adam and Eve. He chose Abraham, Jacob, Moses. He chose the nation of Israel, calling her to Himself again and again despite her betrayal. He came even closer in the person of Jesus Christ, literally "God with us." John the disciple wrote with awe, "The Word became flesh and made his dwelling among us" (John 1:14). God walked with us, getting His feet dusty. He endured the hot sun with us, enjoyed the cool breeze with us, and, exhausted, slept beside us. We heard His laugh, saw His anger, felt His touch. We sat at the table with Him, talking late into the night over wine, bread, bitter herbs, and lamb.

In John's culture, the table was a place of communion in its most secular sense—a place of conversation, of exchange between hearts and minds, a place where relationships, sometimes covenants, were established. The meal was simply the vehicle for this interaction. Even today in bedouin culture, a visitor, whether friend or stranger, is welcomed by the immediate setting of the table. The meal is the appetizer, conversation the entrée. To be given a place at the table is an honor that results in some form of communion.

To be given a seat at the right hand of the host is the highest honor. John himself had vied for this place with his own brother, James (see Mark 10:35–45). Jesus rebuked them by saying, "You don't know what you are asking." For in conferring upon them a new status, Jesus also bestowed upon His disciples a new responsibility: The one who truly loves will lay down his life for his friend (John 15:13). Jesus was not only describing the way in which He would soon demonstrate His love; He was also defining the standard by which His friends should—and in fact would—demonstrate their love for Him. The eleven present at the table would later risk their lives in defense of their love for Jesus Christ. (Judas, by this time, had gone out into the night to betray Him.)

This love is not only the standard of friendship with Christ; it is also the standard of friendship with another believer. "My command is this," Jesus told them: "Love each other as I have loved you" (John 15:12). Our culture sees friendship as a casual option, which is why friends often come and go in our lives. Jesus sees it as an unconditional commitment of selfless love. He can require this of us because He Himself lived it.

True, there is no other god who invites you into his inner circle or says, "Sit by me. Let me tell you my secrets." When Jesus said this to His disciples at the Passover meal, they must have shivered with delight and pride. But to be called into Jesus' inner circle is not a matter of status. To say, "I am a friend of Christ" is not to be given the best seat, but the lowest, because that is where He Himself sat. It is not to be given a crown, but a cross. To be chosen as Christ's friend is to be invited into the fellowship of suffering, the fellowship of death. The death of pride. The death of wounded feelings, of nursed grudges. The death of my agenda, my expectations. Death to standards of performance. Death to ownership, to turf, to possessions, to status, to what is *mine* and what is *me*.

The New Testament church was a community of

friendship characterized by these acts of dying daily: sharing each other's sorrows, celebrating each other's victories, pooling their possessions, cooperating, forgiving, becoming accountable, preserving unity. "This is how all men will know you are My disciples," Jesus said, "by the way you love each other" (John 13:35). He had a purpose in His plan: not just that in loving we should die, but that in dying we might be born to live in a new way.

Ultimately, to be drawn into friendship with Jesus is to be drawn into the fellowship of His resurrection. Life comes from these acts of death. "I have chosen you for my friends in order that you might bear much fruit," Jesus explained (John 15:16). When we lay down our lives for our friends, there is born in us love, joy, peace, patience. Where there was selfishness and grasping, there is kindness, goodness, faithfulness. Where there was manipulation, there is gentleness and self-control (Gal. 5:22–23). This kind of friendship is ripe, luscious fruit, irresistible to others. Ultimately, our friendships draw others to Christ, and that is the fruit we were appointed to bear, the fruit that lasts. That is the purpose for which He draws us to His side and to each other.

"Love for God is not something sentimental or emotional," wrote Oswald Chambers. "For a saint to love as God loves is the most practical thing imaginable." Jesus never intended friendship—with Him or with others—to be a concept, but a way of life. "I call you friends" is not something to be cross-stitched or set in stained glass, but something to be lived out. By taking up the common elements of a meal, Christ ensured that the sacred would remain interwoven with the secular. "Whenever you do this," He said, "think of Me." Whenever you laugh with a friend. Whenever you sit down to a meal. Whenever you have a conversation. Whenever you must lay down your life in some day-to-day form.

*W*omen have the advantage in this format of friendship. The traditional roles or activities assigned to women are servant roles: caregiver, teacher, arbiter, counselor, nurturer. These are the very things that should make us good at being Christlike friends. Cook, cleaning woman, seamstress, gardener, household manager—these are practical ways to be a friend. That we are also creative, intuitive, resourceful multi-taskers makes us even better candidates for true lay-down-your-life-daily friendship. Journalists Ellen Goodman and Patricia O'Brien, writing about their own friendship in their book *I Know Just What You Mean*, note that "women develop *in* relationship, *through* connection. Women don't 'find' themselves or 'understand' themselves all alone but by interacting with others. They forge and reforge their own identity in concert with others, engaged in a long dance of mutuality."

The idea that human maturity is marked by separating—by growing increasingly independent—is one that is a traditionally male model. Men are raised to be strong, self-contained, self-driven, to control their emotions. To men, growing up means growing away—pulling away from parents to stand on your own. But in the late 20th century, a growing number of studies in human development began to challenge the idea that women also grow up by separating from relationships. In fact women do not, in the words of Goodman and O'Brien, "arrive at a static state of adulthood and say to themselves, 'Well, that's that.'" Women are daughters, wives, mothers, friends, co-workers—often all at the same time. Ask a woman who she is, and she will most often define herself in terms of her many relationships: I am a wife, a sister, a mentor.

That women can, and do, define themselves within the context of community—that they can integrate the many facets of their lives into one self—provides an excellent foundation for Christian friendship, for God integrates, not compartmentalizes, life. Has it ever occurred to you how much of Jesus' ministry took place around cooking or eating? While walking? During weddings and visits to His friends? In one of His last earthly moments, walking with two people on the road to Emmaus, Jesus discussed with profound insight God's history with mankind. Yet it was that evening, in the simple breaking and blessing of bread, that they actually recognized Him. This happens to us often in daily life—across the cup of coffee, we suddenly see the presence of Christ in our friend, our child, our neighbor. The Book of Common Prayer captures this moment beautifully in its daily Evening Prayer: "Be our companion in the way, kindle our hearts, and awaken hope, that we may know you as you are revealed in Scripture and the breaking of bread."

Jesus was Himself defined by relationships: brother, cousin, friend, neighbor, teacher, citizen, son of Mary, the Son of God. To accompany Him in His public ministry, Jesus chose for Himself twelve friends. Within that circle, He developed a core of close, trusted companions to whom He disclosed Himself further, upon whom He relied for prayer at the most crucial moment of His life. He was a man to whom people were very important, yet no person deterred Him from faithfulness to His purpose. By looking at Jesus' life, we can learn a great deal about the purpose and place of human relationships in our lives.

Jesus' primary relationship was with His heavenly Father. The story found in Luke 2:40–52 shows us He had established this priority at an early age. At age twelve, Jesus was in the temple amazing the teachers with his understanding of God's Word. And when His worried parents found Him, He said, "Why were you searching for me? Didn't you know I had to be in my Father's house?"

Notice the frame around this story. "And the child grew and became strong; he was filled with wisdom, and the grace of God was upon him" (v. 40). "And Jesus grew in wisdom and stature, and in favor with God and men" (v. 52). The information included at both its beginning and end is that Jesus grew in wisdom. The Greek word for wisdom used here is *sophia*, which means skill, the skill of living an orderly and successful life. Even at age twelve, Jesus was already filled with this skill. His priorities were a result of this wisdom.

Where does one acquire this kind of skill at living? "The fear of the LORD is the beginning of wisdom; all who follow his precepts have good understanding" (Psalm 111:10).

The Hebrew word for wisdom, *chokmah*, also connotes skill, a wisdom that is learned. It is learned by first grasping the fear of the Lord. And what is the fear of the Lord? It is understanding God's place: first and above all. This was what Jesus understood and why He responded with surprise to His mother, "Didn't you know I would be, first and above all, about my Father's business?"

Christ set the same priority for His followers: "'Love the Lord your God with all your heart and with all your soul and with all your mind.' This is the first and greatest commandment" (Matt. 22:37–38). God first, above all. This is an intentional way of living. The demands of daily life do not make it easy. It's not our first response to turn to God, but to turn to the others who bang at our door. But Jesus did not make His statement in a vacuum. He understands what it's like to deal with others' expectations, because His disciples had their own agendas for Him. He understands how hard it is to get away and be alone with God, because people tugged at His cloak all the time. Once when Jesus and His disciples took a boat to get away, the crowd ran around the lake to wait for them on the other side! (See Mark 6:30–34.) Jesus understands that it is not our natural response to put God first. But it can be a learned response. We can learn it from Jesus Himself.

In her book *Between Walden and the Whirlwind: The Key to Life in an Overwhelming World*, Jean Fleming finds this lesson in a small but crucial passage that sums up Jesus' decisive lifestyle: "But Jesus often withdrew to lonely places and prayed" (Luke 5:15). The key words for our consideration are *but* and *often*. "*But* indicates an effort exerted against the pervading pressures. Jesus didn't subject himself to the whims of man. He didn't just flow with the tide. Unlike a leaf carried along by the water, Jesus made choices. Despite the opportunities for service, he chose to withdraw. *Often* indicates habit, custom, pattern. Jesus *often* withdrew to pray."

God must be first, above all, because when this relationship is in sync, all the others will follow. When I am faithful to God, I will be faithful to others. Conversely, when I am unfaithful to God, I will be unfaithful to others. If my relationship to God is out of sync, my other relationships will soon begin to fall apart.

My love for others flows out of my love for God. My respect for others flows out of my respect for God. I humble myself for those I love because of my humility before God. The character required to carry out Christlike relationships is developed only by being obedient to God. The attitudes required to exhibit Christ in my relationships are developed by being in God's presence, being taught by Him and changed by Him. Therefore, my first priority must be my relationship with my heavenly Father. And that means setting limits on the demands made by the other relationships in my life.

*J*esus not only redefined our relationship with God; He redrew the boundaries of human relationships. Consider these passages.

Citizenship:

> Then the Pharisees went out and laid plans to trap him in his words. They sent their disciples to him along with the Herodians. "Teacher," they said, "we know you are a man of integrity and that you teach the way of God in accordance with the truth. You aren't swayed by men, because you pay no attention to who they are. Tell us then, what is your opinion? Is it right to pay taxes to Caesar or not?"
>
> But Jesus, knowing their evil intent, said, "You hypocrites, why are you trying to trap me? Show me the coin used for paying

the tax." They brought him a denarius, and he asked them, "Whose portrait is this? And whose inscription?"

"Caesar's," they replied.

Then he said to them, "Give to Caesar what is Caesar's, and to God what is God's." —Matthew 22:15–21

Family:

Anyone who loves his father or mother more than me is not worthy of me; anyone who loves his son or daughter more than me is not worthy of me; and anyone who does not take his cross and follow me is not worthy of me. —Matthew 10:37–38

Jesus entered a house, and again a crowd gathered, so that he and his disciples were not even able to eat. When his family heard about this, they went to take charge of him, for they said, "He is out of his mind." . . . Then Jesus' mother and brothers arrived. Standing outside, they sent someone in to call him. A crowd was sitting around him, and they told him, "Your mother and brothers are outside looking for you."

"Who are my mother and my brothers?"

he asked.

Then he looked at those seated in a circle around him and said, "Here are my mother and my brothers! Whoever does God's will is my brother and sister and mother." —Mark 3:20–21, 31–35

Near the cross of Jesus stood his mother, his mother's sister, Mary the wife of Clopas, and Mary Magdalene. When Jesus saw his mother there, and the disciple whom he loved standing nearby, he said to his mother, "Dear woman, here is your son," and to the disciple, "Here is your mother." From that time on, this disciple took her into his home. —John 19:25–27

Friend:

Greater love has no one than this, that he lay down his life for his friends. You are my friends if you do what I command. I no longer call you servants, because a servant does not know his master's business. Instead, I have called you friends, for everything that I learned from my Father I have made known to you. —John 15:13–15

Jesus was speaking to people whose religion was deeply ingrained in their culture. He knew that in choosing to follow Him, many would be disowned by their families, abandoned by their friends, arrested and persecuted by their government—even by the leaders of their own religious establishment. For these first followers, the other believers would be their only family, their only friends. Even so, Jesus' teachings on relationships were stunningly radical—to some, subversive. But read them carefully. Nowhere does Jesus say, "Do not care for your mother or brother. Turn your back on your friends." On the contrary, He lovingly redefined the shape of family when from the cross He saw to it that both His mother and His best friend had someone to belong to. Neither does Jesus ever say, "Overthrow your government." Of all these relationships, Jesus merely says, "Give them their due. But give God His due." God first, above all.

If God is first in our affections, God's purpose will be first on our agendas. And this will manifest itself in our relationships, just as it did in Christ's. Ultimately, there will come a moment when God's purpose conflicts with our friend's agenda, and we will have to choose. This happened to Jesus Himself. The story is found in John 11:

> **Now a man named Lazarus was sick. He was from Bethany, the village of Mary and her sister Martha. This Mary, whose brother Lazarus now lay sick, was the same one who**

poured perfume on the Lord and wiped his feet with her hair. So the sisters sent word to Jesus, "Lord, the one you love is sick."

Jesus' response is baffling:

When he heard this, Jesus said, "This sickness will not end in death. No, it is for God's glory so that God's Son may be glorified through it." Jesus loved Martha and her sister and Lazarus. Yet when he heard that Lazarus was sick, he stayed where he was two more days.

Did you catch that? Jesus loved Martha, Mary, and Lazarus—yet when He heard that Lazarus was sick, *He stayed where He was two more days.* It took the messenger several days to reach Jesus with the news, then Jesus waited two more days, and it took several more days to journey with the messenger to Bethany, so by the time Jesus arrived, Lazarus had died—and not just in the last few minutes, but long enough ago that the burial had already taken place. Lazarus had been, according to custom, basted with spices, wrapped in cloth, and sealed in a cave, left to bake in the hot sun of the Middle Eastern desert. When Jesus arrived, Lazarus was, well . . . *well done* (pardon my pun). And the two sisters were fit to be tied. You can tell they had been fretting about it together, because they both said the same thing, even though they came to meet Jesus separately: "Lord, if You had been here, this would not have happened."

I can't tell you how many times I have wagged my finger at God and said, "If You had done what I wanted, things would have turned out differently." At those times, Jesus has drawn His boundaries with me as heartbreakingly as He did with Martha. "Jesus said to her, 'Your brother will rise again.' Martha answered, 'I know he will rise again in the resurrection at the last day.' Jesus said to her, 'I am the resurrection and the life. He who believes in me will live, even though he dies; and whoever lives and believes in me will never die. Do you believe this?'" Martha pussy-foots around this question. "'Yes, Lord,' she told him, 'I believe that you are the Christ, the Son of God, who was to come into the world.'"

That's not what He'd asked. Jesus had said, "Martha, I have the power over life and death. Do you trust Me with it?" And she did not.

I wonder if Jesus wept at this point because His own best friends still didn't get it. Or perhaps He wept because He truly did love Mary, Martha, and Lazarus, and was sorry they had to go through such pain in order to accomplish God's purpose. In any case, Jesus stood before Lazarus' tomb and proved that He did, in fact, have the power over life and death. Imagine the surprise when Jesus commanded Lazarus to come out and Lazarus obeyed (John 11:38–44)!

Many of the people standing by wondered aloud why Jesus had not come sooner, if He had this power. Couldn't He have healed Lazarus, sparing His friends the pain of death? Why put them through this if He loved them? You and I can understand why if we go back and look at Jesus' original response when word came that Lazarus was sick: "When he heard this, Jesus said, 'This sickness will not end in death. No, it is for God's glory so that God's Son may be glorified through it'" (John 11:4).

Yes, Jesus loved His friends, but Jesus' first priority was not to spare His friends pain. Jesus loved His disciples, who did not want Him to go to Bethany, because it was too dangerous. But Jesus' first priority was not His disciples' comfort. Jesus' priority was His Father: first, above all. He looked first to His Father. He listened for His Father to say, "Go." Because He did, watch what resulted: "Therefore many of the Jews who had come to visit Mary, and had seen what Jesus did, put their faith in him" (John 11:45).

If God is first, above all in my affections, His purpose will be first, above all on my agenda. Jesus obeyed God first, above all, even when it cost His friend's life. Not only this, but Jesus obeyed God first, above all, even when it required His own life.

> **Your attitude should be the same as that of Christ Jesus: Who, being in very nature God, did not consider equality with God**

something to be grasped, but made himself nothing, taking the very nature of a servant, being made in human likeness. And being found in appearance as a man, he humbled himself and became obedient to death—even death on a cross! Therefore God exalted him to the highest place and gave him the name that is above every name, that at the name of Jesus every knee should bow, in heaven and on earth and under the earth, and every tongue confess that Jesus Christ is Lord, to the glory of God the Father.

—Philippians 2:5–11

Notice two very important things about this passage: First, that because Christ put God first, above all, God's purpose in Christ was accomplished.

Second, notice that *our attitude should be the same as that of Christ Jesus.* We must want what He wanted: God's purpose accomplished. And we must be willing to lay down our lives for that purpose. Paul went on to encourage his friends in Philippi, "It is God who works in you to will and to act according to his good purpose" (v. 13). His purpose for us, as we have learned, is that we all attain to full maturity, becoming just like Christ. Because that is His purpose in your life, it must be *my* purpose in your life. And I must be willing to lay down my life in order to see it accomplished.

How can you, my friend in the faith, help me to become more like Christ? You can know me. You can be there. Hold me accountable for holy living. Encourage me to live the life of the Spirit. Model servanthood. Keep me active in worship and service. And you can do all this in the course of our days and years together, not just doing *holy* things, but understanding that all the things we do hold the possibility of the holy.

For we do have rituals of friendship, little ceremonies that women carve out of life. We begin as girls trading clothes, trading stories, telling secrets. We help each other move from college dorm to first apartment, from bridal shower to baby shower, from the assistant's desk to the corner office, the corner office to the home office. We steal away for afternoons of shopping, for weekends at the beach. There we are by each other's side in snapshot after snapshot, through hemlines and hairstyles, weddings and birthdays, graduations and funerals. These moments are our communion, and in them Christ is present. We know Him in the words that are spoken and the breaking of bread. And slowly but surely, along the journey, He changes us.

Chapter Two
Know Me

I'm an open book to you . . .
—Psalm 139:2 The Message

How do we become friends? We meet by the neighborhood pool, watching our kids splash. On the day you move in next door, the day I sit down by you in law school or in the waiting room of the oncologist's office. We negotiate a merger or plan a class picnic. We might meet through mutual acquaintances . . .

"You have so much in common!"

"She's a teacher, too."

"You're both newlyweds!"

"This is my friend I was telling you about . . ."

And maybe we do have so much in common—or just enough to get us started on the road from acquaintance to friend.

As women, we embark on this journey by telling each other our stories. We talk. We chit-chat. We commiserate. We laugh. Nothing earth-shattering may be said, but the talk is important. As my friend Peggy Benson says, "No talk is too small." Talk is the first dance of friendship between two women.

In their book, *I Know Just What You Mean*, Ellen Goodman and Patricia O'Brien write: "Talk is at the very heart of women's friendships, the core of the way women connect. It's the given, the absolute assumption of friendship . . . a living current of conversation. . . . Talk is what we all take for granted and yet it is precisely what makes women value and feel valued in friendships. In these on-going dialogues, women reveal themselves. Gradually, trust is tested and won; an intimate comfort zone is created. Women know this intuitively—and they've had the language to express it for a long time."

Talk is also what we have the least time for—real, long, uninterrupted talk, the chance to lavish attention solely on one person, to hear and be heard.

Several years ago, my husband and I hosted a conference for ministers and their wives. Dennis planned the husbands' track, and I planned for the wives. Comparing our schedules, Dennis noted that I had nothing on the wives' schedule the second afternoon. No meetings. No sightseeing. He wondered what we were going to do.

"Talk," I said. "We'll have coffee available, and there are sofas and chairs."

"Talk?" he replied, astounded. "Just *talk*? For three hours?"

I thought for a moment.

"You're right," I said. "Three hours is probably not enough time."

Dennis didn't understand that "just talk" is serious business to women. Conversation is the place where women do the work of their lives, the growing, the understanding, the reflection. We know that the cocktail party question "So how are you?" when posed by a friend, is not trivial. It's the open door, the invitation, the initial parlay. We know we now have the opportunity—and freedom—to launch into the deep end if we need to. Our girlfriend will go with us. We also know we must choose whether to avoid the deep end. So if we are having a bad day and don't want to discuss it, "How are you?" can be a loaded question, the hardest question to answer. That's precisely why it is such a crucial one for us to ask each other. And when you ask, be ready to listen. When women talk—about our children, our work, our dress size—what we are really saying is, "Know me." Which is another way of saying, "Help me figure out who I am."

Ellen Goodman and Patricia O'Brien write, "When

children—especially girls on their way to becoming women—are ready for change, they often look to friends to see who they really are, or who they are becoming. During adolescence, girls most urgently and famously need someone to see them not as they are, but as they want to be."

I have two vivid memories of my first days at college. The first is the moment my parents hugged me, stepped into the family car, and drove away, leaving me on the side steps of Collins dormitory. I sat on the steps, hugging my knees and choking back tears. At least that's how I remember it; maybe that's just what I felt like doing. What I do remember is watching that car carrying the two people who gave me my identity take that identity away with them. There went my childhood, down the road, around the corner. Left on the steps was . . . who? I did not know yet. I felt profoundly lonely—and the person I missed most was me.

I climbed the steps back up to the second floor dorm room, where my best friend Nancy Lewis sat on one of our matching twin green bedspreads. "Did you cry?" she asked. I nodded. "So did I," she answered. Together we went down the hall, making acquaintances of other girls, one of whom had a car. We piled into it, driving up and down the unfamiliar streets of Waco, Texas, getting our bearings—ostensibly looking for some place to eat. What we were really looking for was some place to belong.

The second big college moment I remember came as

I was walking across the lawn after the first day of class. Other students headed out to classes, practices, the cafeteria, or the library, pushing past me. And it hit me like a thunderbolt: These people don't know who I am. I wasn't the smartest or prettiest or most popular girl in my high school, but I distinguished myself. In my youth group at church, I was a leader. I grew up with the same kids in the same neighborhood since first grade. We were Camp Fire Girls together. We slathered each other with suntan lotion, shared the same pink frosted lipstick, pierced our ears, and dedicated "Close To You" to our current boyfriends on KVIL radio. None of these people at college knew any of that. They had whole histories of their own, histories in which I had no part, of which they were the center.

What I realized that afternoon on the lawn—had begun to understand earlier on the steps—was that life had forever and irretrievably changed. I was no longer the *me* I had been. At that moment I was, in fact, nobody. Whoever I was going to be, she was out there among these strangers, among whoever would become my friends. It was time to write a new chapter of history, and I had no idea who the characters in my story would be, or where and when I would find them.

I did find my new self along with my new friends. Together we launched into the brave new world of *us*. Some of us have traveled together on the journey of life and faith, work and child-raising, health crises and midlife crises in the twenty-five years since. I still discover new worlds in new friends, but when I really need to know myself, I turn back to the ones who have been there.

George Herbert wrote that the best mirror is an old friend. You need friends who have known you before a marriage, a career, an illness, a crisis, a bad habit—people who can identify your true and best self, the qualities that have made you who you are throughout your whole life. What truest part of you do you want to retain and carry away from the present circumstance? What part of you has been changed by it in a way that you want to carry its benefit into the next phase of life?

This is an important function of friends: the good ones know us. They know our stories; most likely they were there when the stories happened. They help us to know where we fit, like a jigsaw piece that needs the rest of the puzzle for context.

My friend is my totem, my historian, my library of memory. My friend serves as my navigation point, by which I know my place in the world. A true friend, one who walks worthy, is a rudder. She keeps me from drifting off course. I need my friend to be what Ellen Goodman calls "a steady anchor to myself."

My friend reminds me of where I came from:

> I have been reminded of your sincere faith, which first lived in your grandmother Lois and in your mother Eunice and, I am persuaded, now lives in you also.
> —2 Timothy 1:5

. . . and who I am now:

> For this reason I remind you to fan into flame the gift of God, which is in you through the laying on of my hands.
> —2 Timothy 1:6

. . . and who I am called to be:

> For God did not give us a spirit of timidity, but a spirit of power, of love and of self-discipline.
> —2 Timothy 1:7

The young pastor Timothy had this voice of truth in his mentor and friend, the apostle Paul. The young queen Esther had her cousin Mordecai. Forced to choose between a personal and a national crisis, it was Mordecai who reminded Esther: this is who you are (Esther 3:7–4:17). In a crucial moment, she turned for advice to someone who shared her identity, her history, and her values.

"Women do friendship differently than men," Patricia O'Brien and Ellen Goodman observe. "Among women, friendship is conducted face-to-face. While women tend to *be* together, men tend to *do* together. . . . Men's friendships are based on shared activities, women's on shared feelings. Men put shared interests highest among the reasons they bond with a friend, while women first want friends who share their values."

There is great comfort in having someone who knows who you are, because when you are not yourself, she recognizes it. "This is not like you," she says. "What's the deal?" At a college reunion, one friend exclaimed to her former roommate, "Where did you get those boobs?" One good friend and I share what we call "thumb sucking days"—those days when life overwhelms us, when we just want to lie under the covers in a fetal position. We have come to recognize those signs in each other, to know when it is time to come over, get the other one dressed, and go for a walk or a movie.

Friends not only know where we have come from, they know what we have gone through to get there. We know each other's soft spots, and we watch out for each other. We are gentle with each other in the broken places. We know, even anticipate, when we should tiptoe softly, when the other will need to walk slowly. We watch each other's backs. In my circle of friends, there are some unspoken rules: no blind dates for one friend. For another friend, no movies where the dad deserts the family. No claustrophobic spaces for me. I can't tell you how many times my friends have been in small hot rooms and said to each other, "I am so glad Karla isn't here!"

Friends know what needs to be celebrated—the small acts of courage, moments that appear insignificant to others, but are actually big personal victories. I know how much courage it took my friend to visit the dad who deserted her. She knows how much will-power it takes for me to pass up a basket of chips or a plate of brownies. We have one friend who cannot refuse anything that is asked of her. Every committee that needs a chairman, every event that needs to be planned, every children's choir to be led—she is a sucker for it. The first time she actually turned down a request, we all took her to dinner and awarded her a "Just Say No" ribbon. Are all these equally devastating issues? Maybe not, but in friendship, they are equally celebrated.

Friends know when we need to laugh at ourselves, to take ourselves less seriously. I have a funny friend who will listen to my rant, lean across the table sympathetically, and say, "Karla, look at it this way." Then with a straight face, she will tilt her head to look at the world sideways. I have seen this joke a hundred times, but it never fails to restore my perspective. Coming from someone else, it would not be effective. This friend has been there through other rants, other conflicts, and other resolutions. She has earned the right to say, "Lighten up." Every time she tilts her head sideways, she reminds me of past crises that are long resolved. When I lose my perspective, I need someone with the same history, just a different view. At that moment when I have lost it, there is no gift greater than someone who can say, "Honey, remember when . . ."

Inside jokes are part of that bank of memory. In my work as a writer and speaker, I travel frequently. When I travel I am hardly ever alone, but I am often lonely. The people I am with may be nice people, but they are new people. I miss having someone who gets the private jokes—what my son calls "location jokes." You have to have "been there" to get it. A good friend is someone who was there. I was there at the beach the weekend my four friends and I decided to purchase straw hats and discovered that no matter how glamorous a straw hat she wears, my red-headed, freckled friend Vicki looks just like Huck Finn. Now every time we pass a rack of straw hats, we have to stop and try one on Vicki. No words are necessary. We dissolve into tears of laughter. People look at us strangely in Wal-mart.

My friend Saralu is famous for her "Saralu moments." Like the Christmas she gave my boys walkie talkies that we couldn't get to work.

"Maybe they need batteries," we suggested.

"I don't think so," Saralu replied. "They're General Electric."

At friends-and-family gatherings, we sometimes entertain ourselves by recounting our favorite "Saralu moments." Sara graciously tolerates this teasing. It is our way of laying claim to her, of saying "I was there." That we were there is a thing to brag about, because to be Saralu's friend is to be in a lucky group. She is that one friend in a million. I know because she is my friend.

For any of us, to have such a friend is to be in a lucky group. To have a true friend is to be chosen and to feel that chosenness. "Know me" is the cry of a woman's heart. To want to know and be known is a God-like quality. God wants to be known. In the cool of the evening, He would walk with Adam and Eve in the garden. And what would they do? Talk. God loves to reveal Himself; women get that quality from Him. It is a part of being made in His likeness. "In the image of God, male and female He created them," and for the most part, women reflect that side of God which seeks relationship through the revelation of self to self.

"I know you," is the astonishing, dreadful, wonderful statement God makes to man.

"You know me!" man exclaims—and this leaves us at once feeling cherished while shaking in our boots. Revelation is an act of faith. It is a leap off the cliff. To reveal yourself is to leave yourself wide open. To be known is to lay aside your shield, step from behind the curtain, relinquish your invincibility—to open your hands, knowing that they may be pierced by nails. To know and be known is to be like Christ.

When you engage in this kind of friendship, you ensure yourself pain. You will be wounded, sometimes unintentionally. Sometimes for your own good.

"Pat tells me that I have an overdeveloped sense of responsibility, as if life were a dinner party and I were the hostess," Ellen Goodman says of her best friend.

"I didn't know I was hard to get along with; I didn't know I was irritable; I didn't know I was selfish. Nobody told me," says Bible teacher Joyce Meyer. It takes a true friend to tell you the hard truths. And yes, that will hurt. But only the truth will set you free. "Truth, like surgery, may hurt, but it cures," wrote the Chinese physician Han Suyin. To love your friend enough to put your finger in the place it will hurt is to love her as Christ loves.

Mark 10:17–22 tells the story of a rich young ruler who experienced this painful truth-telling love. "I have kept all Your laws," he said proudly to Jesus. Then, "Jesus looked at him and loved him. 'One thing you lack,' he said. 'Go, sell everything you have and give to the poor, and you will have treasure in heaven. Then come, follow me'" (Mark 10:21).

"Jesus looked at him," Mark noted. When Jesus looks at us, He reads us like a book. He sees us completely. He doesn't just glance. He knows us. This is frightening. Scholars believe that Mark's Gospel recorded Peter's account of Jesus' ministry. If so, it is interesting that Mark made this note about the rich young ruler, that Jesus looked at him, because Peter himself would have experienced this same look.

"I will never desert you!" Peter had boldly declared.

Jesus looked at him and predicted accurately, "Before the cock crows tomorrow morning, you will have denied Me three times" (Mark 14:30).

Later, Peter had stood shuffling his sandals in the dust, avoiding the look in Jesus' eyes when He asked, "Peter, do you love Me?" It is so hard to have someone look at you and see right through you. But notice what Mark goes on to say regarding the rich young ruler: "Jesus looked at him *and loved him.*"

He loved him in spite of, even because of, what He saw. That is the way God loves. God showed His great love for us in that while we were yet sinners Christ died for us (Rom. 5:8). God loves us even with our shortcomings, but He wants our good, which is our full maturity. That is why He sent Christ. No one is righteous; no one measures up (Rom. 3:23). So God made Him who had no sin to be sin for us, so that in Him we might become the righteousness of God (2 Cor. 5:21). God loves us as we are, but He does not leave us as we are. Because Jesus loved him, He identified what the young man needed. He said, "Here's what you lack." When Jesus looks at me, He reads me completely, loves me as I am, and confronts me about what is lacking.

God confronts and challenges *because* He loves us enough to want us to grow beyond what we are lacking into full maturity. He calls us to love each other in the same way.

> **Then we will no longer be infants, tossed back and forth by the waves, and blown here and there by every wind of teaching and by the cunning and craftiness of men in their deceitful scheming. Instead, speaking the truth in love, we will in all things grow up into him who is the Head, that is, Christ. From him the whole body, joined and held together by every supporting ligament, grows and builds itself up in love, as each part does its work.** —Ephesians 4:14–16

This was Paul's goal for the friends he loved: "Night and day we pray most earnestly that we may see you again and *supply what is lacking in your faith*" (1 Thess. 3:10). A true friend knows me and loves me as I am, but she wants more for me. She wants for me what is lacking in Christlike maturity, precisely because it is what Jesus Himself wants. What might have happened if this rich young man had a group of friends who insisted, "But you *must* listen to Him. You must do what He said!"

For many years, Jesus has spoken to me about personal disciplines that were lacking in my faith. One of them was weight control. Like this young man, I did not listen—even when my weight caused serious health issues. What finally caused me to take Him seriously was the invitation from my missionary friend to come to her area and bring a team of women who would prayerwalk. Literally, we would walk through villages that had not opened up to any missionaries yet. No Christian had ever been there! We would go in, walk around, and pray that God would open this place and send workers to live here.

The trip would be difficult. My doctor said, "You cannot go." It was an awful realization: I could not follow where Jesus was leading because of the one thing I lacked. I was heart-broken—enough to finally do something about my health. With my doctor's supervision, I began a serious diet and exercise program. I went into training. And my friends rallied around me. One of them called me every day: "Have you walked?" She came to my house and walked with me, despite her busy schedule. When it got so hot in the summer that I could not stand to walk, one friend brought over her treadmill—not a small treadmill, but the big official one. A friend trained me in working with weights. Another, a nutritionist, supervised my diet. My friends embraced and encouraged my journey as I followed and obeyed Christ.

One of the hardest but most necessary things I did was to ask for prayer support in this process. I ruthlessly stomped on my pride and e-mailed eight women I love and respect—respect enough to make myself accountable to them. All eight of them are serious pray-ers. I did not need friends who would think of me fondly every now and then; I needed women who were skilled in intercession. Paul described such a friend in Colossians 4:12: "He is always wrestling in prayer for you, that you may stand firm in all the will of God, mature and fully assured." I needed professional wrestlers.

James encouraged the believers in Jerusalem to be this kind of friend to each other:

> **Is any one of you sick? He should call the elders of the church to pray over him and anoint him with oil in the name of the Lord. And the prayer offered in faith will make the sick person well; the Lord will raise him up. If he has sinned, he will be forgiven. Therefore confess your sins to each other and pray for each other so that you may be healed. The prayer of a righteous man is powerful and effective. —James 5:14–16**

The kind of sickness James describes is "sick from sin." I was literally sick from sin. I confessed my sin to this group of eight women. It was not easy! These are all strong, capable women in professional Christian ministry—women who are mature in the faith and who (I assume) think I am mature in the faith. I had to admit to them my immaturity.

They responded with grace and fierceness. They took my request seriously, e-mailing me daily, weekly to ask, "How are you doing?" They asked for specific progress reports, not just a general "I'm doing fine." Most importantly, they told me specific Scripture passages and prayer requests on my behalf. "I walk every morning," one friend wrote, "and I always tell God to get you out of bed to walk." My favorite note of encouragement was this: "Every time I lift my fork, I ask God to keep you from lifting yours!"

It was a group project. And in the end, there was group delight. When I finally walked the streets of that village and prayed, they could not have been more present with me if they were physically standing there. "Girls," I whispered, "I made it."

Understand something: I have never asked for help like this before. As a result, I never got it. I never knew the power and joy—the freedom—that can be given by friends who know all, love all, and bear all.

Do you want your friend to deliver the truth? Some women don't. And some women don't want the responsibility to tell the truth. Because I eat with them all the time, I gave my closest friends the freedom to say, "Don't eat that," when I reached for the basket of chips or ordered dessert. "I don't want to tell her that," one friend said. "I might hurt her feelings."

Yes, it might. It did, even though I had given my friends permission to say those things. The truth is hard to hear and even harder to deliver. It rocks boats, topples illusions—it makes us uncomfortable. And women are raised to be nice. We're taught to be polite, to get along. In fact, women are put in charge of making sure everyone gets along, that no feathers get ruffled, that everyone has a good time. All this comes at a great cost.

"If I avoided confronting her," Ellen Goodman wrote of her friend, "she and I might lose something fundamental: our trust in each other to deliver the truth."

My trust in you runs all the way from, "That color doesn't look good on you," to "This habit is destroying you." If we travel together very far on the journey of faith, we will see both the good and bad side of each other. I will see my friend's best moments and her worst. I will be disappointed in her, even angry with her.

"Anger with a friend is a surprise," says Goodman. "Women act as if in a good friendship, there shouldn't be anything to be angry about, that the absence of anger is what makes friendship safe—safer than marriages or family relationships. . . . When two friends allow themselves to express their feelings honestly, even when those feelings include anger, that is itself an act of trust."

The novelist Harriet Beecher Stowe wrote, "Truth is the kindest thing we can give folks in the end." Truth sets people free. By it, "we will in all things grow up into him who is the Head, that is, Christ," Paul wrote to his friends in Ephesus (Eph. 4:15). But Paul instructed his friends to speak the truth in love. Paul went on in Ephesians 4 to list all kinds of behaviors about which his friends should confront each other. But he summed up his instructions with this final exhortation: "Be kind and compassionate to one another, forgiving each other, just as in Christ God forgave you" (Eph. 4:32).

"The truth is not simply what you think it is," Vaclav Havel, president of the Czech Republic, once said. "It is also the circumstances in which it is said, and to whom, why, and how it is said." I gave my friends permission to say those hard things to me. They were spoken in love by women who know me well. They know that I value the truth at all costs. They understood what was at stake—not only my physical health, but my spiritual health as well. Not one of them spoke cruelly, although many of them said hard things. Some of them spoke with their actions. Some spoke with prayer and some with Scripture. All of them had one goal—that I would grow in Christ—and what I heard from each of them was love.

Gary Smalley identifies what he calls the Five Love Languages—the differing ways in which people hear loved expressed. Some people respond best to words of affirmation. These people will do anything to hear someone say, "Good job," or "I'm proud of you." When this person tells you she loves you, she says, "You're smart, or pretty, or funny." Some people respond best to acts of service. For them, love is something you do. They speak lovingly by saying, "How can I help you?" For others, love is expressed through quality time. This friend needs you to do things with her, give her your full attention. You may have a friend who expresses love through physical touch: hugs, tickles, a pat on the back, a poke in the ribs, a hand to hold. And some friends speak the language of love by receiving and giving gifts—surprises, indulgences, little things that make you feel special.

It is possible that I may *be* loved, but not *feel* loved because my friend is not speaking my language. A friend may have her own way of expressing love, but she will also learn the language of my heart and speak it fluently.

At some point in a true relationship, we choose to be this kind of journey-friend: We choose to know each other this well. A friendship, like any other relationship, has its stages. We meet. We are attracted to each other. We fall in love. Telling my story is a part of the falling-in-love stage. Watch two people out together in the early stages of dating. They are talking, eye-to-eye, fascinated with each other, telling their stories, the jokes that the other has never heard them tell before, the little anecdotes.

Some people can't get beyond this telling-my-story stage. But there is a point at which it's time to write "the rest of the story"—the point at which you choose to go on, to travel together. It is the point that requires adjusting to each other and for each other—the point at which *my* story and *your* story become *our* story. People fall in love, but if you intend to stay, eventually you choose to love.

One of the choices you make is to listen to your friend. There is "a time to be silent and a time to speak," says the teacher in Ecclesiastes 3:7. It's interesting that men have to reach a comfortable level of intimacy in order to talk to someone else. Women have to reach a comfortable level of intimacy before they can be silent. Women talk most when they are nervous. We talk to cover the silence—to avoid leaving open that space which allows for someone else's acceptance or rejection. Two women who can walk down a path together in silence most likely have a long history together. They have ease.

One afternoon my friend Kim and I went climbing at a local nature preserve. We hiked to the top of a ridge on a beautiful spring day. There was not another soul around. At the top of the ridge was a bench and a field of blue flowers. We sat on the bench for half an hour, leaning against each other, not saying a word. Later that week, Kim sent me a note that said, "A true friend knows how to sit in the sun and shut up."

For all the longings we have to be close to one another, women make each other nervous. We are still basically girls at our first day of school, our first day on the playground, our first day on the campus. You hold within your heart the potential to enlarge me, to empower and enrich me—and the power to wound me. I always know that, and I guard myself against it.

I guard myself in a number of ways—ways that are not beneficial to friendship.

Ellen Goodman and Patricia O'Brien explain, "When a woman talks to a close friend, she anticipates the other person's feelings and, in the process, may begin to pre-edit her own half of the conversation. This is what Judith Jordan calls 'anticipatory empathy.' One person knows—or assumes she knows—how another will feel. The mutual empathy can give women wholly satisfying feelings of understanding and being understood, or it can set up stumbling blocks that make it impossible to talk honestly and directly."

Since we were infants, the people in our lives have had expectations of us. Our parents wanted us to be like them, or to do better than they did. Our teachers wanted us to make good grades, to behave ourselves in the classroom. Coaches wanted us to achieve. Bosses want us to add to the bottom line. A friend ought to provide some relief from this. The last thing we need is more expectation. A friend recognizes and honors your personality without imposing her own.

One of the rules of traveling together must be "Don't *assume* you know me." Assumption is deadly to the process of revelation. It's amazing what happens when you pay attention instead. Listen to the nuances, to what's unspoken. Learn to read me. Good therapists practice this method. Counselor Julie Morgenstern describes the process in *Starting Over (With Dog)*: "I listened quietly, paying attention to her voice and expression. After each possibility, she would give a slight shrug as if to say, 'I don't know what to do.' Yet it seemed to me that she had the answers inside her. When she talked about ideas she liked, her voice was light, her face relaxed, even smiling. With options that didn't sit well, her words and face were strained and heavy."

Writing to his friends in Philippi, Paul said, "This is my prayer: that your love may abound more and more in knowledge and depth of insight" (Phil. 1:9). Paul prayed that they would "not only love much but well" with love that was "sincere and intelligent, not sentimental gush" (*The Message*). That word *intelligent* means "discerning." To listen with discernment is to read between the lines, to hear what is not being said. In his book *Let Your Life Speak*, Parker Palmer describes what happened when his friends listened with this kind of intelligent love as he made a crucial career choice. Offered the presidency of a small educational institution, Palmer called half a dozen trusted friends together, in what is known in the Quaker tradition as a "clearness committee." They didn't offer advice; instead, they asked him questions, listening for the truth of the situation to be revealed. "Halfway into the process, someone asked a question that . . . turned out to be very hard: 'What would you like most about being a president?'" Palmer pondered the question before answering.

"Well, I would not like having to give up my writing and my teaching . . . I would not like the politics of the presidency, never knowing who your real friends are . . . I would not like having to glad-hand people I do not respect simply because they have money . . . I would not like . . ."

Gently but firmly, the person who had posed the question interrupted me: "May I remind you that I asked you what you would most **like**?"

I responded impatiently, "Yes, yes, I'm working my way toward an answer." Then I resumed my sullen but honest litany: "I would not like having to give up my summer vacations . . . I would not like having to wear a suit and tie all the time . . . I would not like . . ."

Once again the questioner called me back to the original question. But this time I felt compelled to give the only honest answer I possessed, an answer that came from the very bottom of my barrel, an answer that appalled me even as I spoke it.

"Well," said I, in the smallest voice I possess, "I guess what I'd like most is getting my picture in the paper with the word **president** under it."

I was sitting with seasoned Quakers who knew that though my answer was laughable, my mortal soul was clearly at stake! They did not laugh at all but went into a long and serious silence—a silence in which I could only sweat and inwardly groan.

Finally my questioner broke the silence with a question that cracked all of us up—and cracked me open: "Parker," he said, "can you think of an easier way to get your picture in the paper?"

Ouch. Also . . . Wow! The power of intelligent love. The gift of having a friend who reads me like a book, a friend who not only says hard things, but asks the hard questions. Imagine what a wrong turn Parker Palmer might have made in his journey of faith if his friend hadn't listened with discernment.

What strikes me about this experience is that this friend heard what Palmer's heart was really saying *and he was not shocked.* He was not accusing. He did not laugh at him but laughed with him. When I asked some of my girlfriends to define a "true friend," they said:

A true friend is . . .
Someone who has seen you try on bathing suits.
Someone who has cleaned your toilet.
Someone who has seen what's under your refrigerator.
Someone who knows how much you weigh.

And everyone of them added,

And she was not shocked.

There it is, the thing that we long for most: someone

who knows us, really knows us, and is not shocked. It is the question we ask our boyfriends and our best friends, the question Carole King expressed so well in a song written 30 years ago: "Will you still love me tomorrow?" Deep in my heart, I am sure that if you really knew me, you would not love me. And to be fair, there are some people who wouldn't. Some people would leave us or laugh at us. Believers are called to a higher standard of friendship. We are called to love as God loves.

"Dear friends, let us love one another, for love comes from God. Everyone who loves has been born of God and knows God. Whoever does not love does not know God, because God is love. This is how God showed his love among us: He sent his one and only Son into the world that we might live through him. This is love: not that we loved God, but that he loved us and sent his Son as an atoning sacrifice for our sins. Dear friends, since God so loved us, we also ought to love one another" (1 John 4:7–11).

"We love because he first loved us," John wrote (1 John 4:19). Our problem with loving others unconditionally is that we are not sure *God* loves us unconditionally. "Love your neighbor as yourself," Jesus said. And most of us do. We love ourselves poorly; therefore we love others poorly. If we apply the same standard of measurement to others that we apply to ourselves, no wonder we do not know how to love others lavishly, as God loves us.

"We know and rely on the love God has for us," says 1 John 4:16. The Greek word translated "rely" is *pisteuo*—to persuade, to have confidence, to believe. If you do not have confidence in God's love for you, perhaps you do not really know Him. God is not shocked by the human heart. He may be disappointed in our behavior, even angered by it, but it does not throw Him for a loop. God was not shocked when Eve chose to reach for the apple. He knew in advance she would do it. When He asked, "What have you done?" He already knew the answer. He stood there while she confronted the truth of her own soul—how easily she had been duped, had disobeyed, had betrayed Him. And then He did not walk away. He made a way. In that moment, God pronounced Eve's salvation: "So the LORD God said to the serpent, 'Because you have done this, cursed are you above all the livestock and all the wild animals! You will crawl on your belly and you will eat dust all the days of your life. And I will put enmity between you and the woman, and between your offspring and hers; he will crush your head, and you will strike his heel'" (Gen. 3:14–15).

God did not curse Eve; He cursed the one who had caused her to sin. The offspring who would crush Satan's head was Jesus Christ. The One who would save her would be born into her own family tree.

What is in our hearts is awful, yes. We know it. As a result, few of us ever let ourselves be known. All our lives we've been hearing things like: What you are thinking or feeling or saying or becoming is stupid or scandalous or shameful or just downright laughable. The voice speaking may have been a parent, a teacher, a spouse, an employer—or just the voice inside our hearts. It doesn't matter. All the infinite variations on them convey just one message: You are not valuable. That is the voice of Satan. It is not the voice of God.

God goes out of His way to demonstrate His love to people who don't deserve it. One of my favorite examples is the story of the Samaritan woman at the well, found in John 4. John begins his account with this statement: "Now he had to go through Samaria."

No, He didn't.

Forty-two miles north of Jerusalem, cutting across the highlands of Israel down to the Jordan River, is a wedge of land that was known as Samaria. The Samaritan people were half-breeds, the descendants of Jews who had intermarried with the many races of people who had conquered them, particularly the Greeks. They offered sacrifices to God at Mount Gerazim, not Jerusalem, and worshiped other gods. For this reason, *true Jews* despised Samaria. In order to travel from Jerusalem in the south to Galilee in the north, a *good* Jew would go miles (and days) out of his way to avoid setting foot on Samaritan soil. So you must catch the irony with which John said, "Now he *had* to go through Samaria."

Why? To be at Jacob's well at the sixth hour—high noon, when no one would be expected to be there. No one except this woman.

She came at that hour because she knew she would be alone. All the other women came in the cool evening, when their work was done, to draw water for the next day and to chat, as women do while they work. No doubt they talked about her, because she had slept with at least six of their husbands by now. This woman knew shame; she knew rejection, and she knew how to hide from it. So she came to the well at noon. And so did God. She left her conversation with Jesus exclaiming, "He knew everything about me!" He also told her about Himself: "Jesus answered her, 'If you knew the gift of God and who it is that asks you for a drink, you would have asked him and he would have given you living water.'

"'Sir,' the woman said, 'you have nothing to draw with and the well is deep. Where can you get this living water? Are you greater than our father Jacob, who gave us the well and drank from it himself, as did also his sons and his flocks and herds?'

"Jesus answered, 'Everyone who drinks this water will be thirsty again, but whoever drinks the water I give him will never thirst. Indeed, the water I give him will become in him a spring of water welling up to eternal life'" (John 4:10–14).

When we become convinced of God's love for us, the wounds, the gaping holes in our hearts become pools of living water through which the water flows over onto someone else. "Whoever believes in me," Jesus said, "streams of living water will flow from within him" (John 7:38). This woman ran back to the very people she most feared. She ran to get them and bring them to Jesus. She was that convinced. Years later, John would write, "This then is how we know that we belong to the truth, and how we set our hearts at rest in his presence whenever our hearts condemn us. For God is greater than our hearts, and he knows everything" (1 John 3:19–20).

I need you, my friend, to know everything, yet love me, because most often I do not love myself. I find myself going to the well at high noon in order to avoid being hurt by anyone who knows me and does not love me. Your acceptance is like cool water poured upon my soul. Until I know in my inner being that I am loved, until I am rooted and established in love, I will not grow to full maturity in God (Eph. 3:16–19).

I need you to know me and love me, because at times I may not even know who I am. You may have to see my potential and call it out of me.

> How great is the love the Father has lavished on us, that we should be called children of God! And that is what we are! *The reason the world does not know us is that it did not know him.* Dear friends, now we are children of God, and

**what we will be has not yet been made
known. But we know that when he appears,
we shall be like him, for we shall see him as
he is.** —1 John 3:1–2

Part of the world is still in me—my human nature.
That part does not recognize who I am in Christ, because
it does not recognize Christ as Lord (1 John 3:1). Plenty
of voices in the world tell me who I am not. I desperately
need someone to remind me who I am in God.

Consider the story of Gideon in Judges 6. Because the
power of nearby Midian was so oppressive, the Israelites
prepared shelters for themselves in mountain clefts,
caves, and strongholds. Whenever we are intimidated or
oppressed, the first thing we do is crawl into our caves,
which we expect to protect us, but which become strongholds in which we are trapped. That's what had happened
to Gideon.

My pastor, Mike Glenn, has helped me to picture
Gideon threshing grain. To thresh grain in that time, you
would need a big, flat, high place called a threshing floor.
You would toss the grain up in the air, and the wind
would blow away the chaff while the grain would fall to
the ground for harvesting. The problem was, the
Midianites would see the Israelites threshing grain up on
their high places, and they would come to take the grain
away. So we find Gideon down in his wine press instead—which was basically a hole in the ground in which

you stomped grapes. Gideon was down in this hole throwing grain around trying to thresh it without being seen because he was afraid of the Midianites. But he was having a very hard time because there was no wind to blow away the chaff. Into this ridiculous scene God's representative came, squatted at the edge of the hole, and called down into it, "Greetings, mighty warrior!"

An unlikely salutation, considering Gideon's behavior. At that point, Gideon didn't feel like a mighty warrior, and he wasn't acting like one. He didn't even know he had the potential. But God did. Sometimes our Father appoints a messenger to come find us and call out our name before we know who we are.

A friend who walks worthy is the friend who will tell me who I am in Christ, even as I am not acting like it—especially when I do not feel it. As soon as we forget our beloved status, we lose our rootedness, our stability, and are easy prey to Satan. The more we grasp our belovedness, the more like Christ we become. He knew who He was because the Father told Him: This is My beloved Son. When Jesus submitted to baptism—necessary for repentance of sins, but unnecessary for the One who was sinless—perhaps in that moment, He was feeling very human. And God said to Him in that moment, "You are divine." As friends who walk worthy, we have the opportunity to speak God's words of love into our friend's life: You are His beloved daughter. We must do this especially when she feels it the least.

"A friend is someone who likes you," wrote the children's writer and illustrator Joan Walsh Anglund. This little book was so precious to me as a girl that I wanted to decorate my bedroom with Anglund's drawings. A great deal of my childhood and adolescence was spent sorting out who really liked me—me, as I was. These girls I understood to be real friends. The others came and went. My mother impressed upon me early and frequently, "Be yourself. Be unique." Uniqueness was valued, therefore friends who accepted—or even applauded—uniqueness were valuable. In fact, they are the only sort of friends to have, but most children can't articulate this. But we do sense it, even as girls. We know who we have to be on guard with, and if we don't, we learn—painfully. The one who doesn't make you over into a suitable companion in her likeness, who doesn't turn on you when it is expedient, who doesn't make fun of you—that is the friend who likes you. Sally Field expressed the cry of our hearts: "You like me! You really like me!" This is quite a trophy.

I decided somewhere around seventh grade that I would only invest in those real friends. If someone didn't like me, I could always find someone else who did. This was my rule. On the occasions that I abandoned it for the favor of the in crowd, I got hurt—hurt enough to remember it even now. For the most part, I went my own way, and it never occurred to me that my way wasn't *the* way. That might have been self-esteem, or it might have been naiveté. Looking back, I see I was on the fringe of the popular group—sometimes in, sometimes not. Probably their mothers made them include me because our mothers were all friends. What matters is that I grew up with this compass: a friend—a real friend—is someone who likes you.

In truth, a real friend is someone who knows you. Sometimes she likes you, but quite frankly, sometimes she doesn't. Sometimes she will not like what she sees, and if she is truly your friend, she will call you on it. She will say, "This is not you." Sometimes she will help you see who you really are, who you don't even know you are yet. Sometimes she will talk, and sometimes she will listen. Sometimes she will applaud you, and sometimes she will rein you in. But always, always, she will love you.

Chapter Three
Be There

I look behind me and you're there, then
up ahead and you're there, too—your
reassuring presence, coming and going.
—Psalm 139:5–6 The Message

I will always, always love Saralu Lunn for many reasons, but Dennis will always love her for this: In 1984, our son Seth was born. His was a particularly traumatic birth. The umbilical cord was wrapped around the baby's neck. With every contraction, his heart rate would plummet. Finally, Seth was born, exhausted. His APGAR rating was pitiful. They let us have a quick look at him, then rushed him to the neonatal unit, with Dennis running alongside the cart. The last words he heard the nurse say were, "No motor reflexes." Then the doors closed behind her, and my husband was left standing alone in the hallway, his son in ICU, his wife in recovery.

At that moment, Saralu Lunn came around the corner.

Presence—it's God's greatest gift to His people. It's what God gave the Israelites: He was in their midst. He camped among them in the wilderness, by day in the form of a cloud that hung over the camp, by night as a pillar of fire. He went before them into battle; they measured their success by it. He dwelt in the temple, within the Holy of Holies. He came to walk among man in the person of Jesus Christ. He lives within believers as the Spirit. God's presence is the greatest blessing He offers His people. It is what we cling to. "Even though I walk through the valley of the shadow of death," David sang, "I will fear no evil, for you are with me" (Psalm 23:4).

"Fear not, for I have redeemed you; I have summoned you by name; you are mine," God promises. "When you pass through the waters, I will be with you" (Isa. 43:1–2). "The Word became flesh and made his dwelling among us," John marveled (John 1:14). In His last moments with His disciples, Jesus promised, "I will ask the Father, and he will give you another Counselor to be with you forever—the Spirit of truth. . . . he lives with you and will be in you. I will not leave you as orphans; I will come to you" (John 14:16–18). At the end of time, this is the joyful announcement: "Now the dwelling of God is with men, and he will live with them. They will be his people, and God himself will be with them and be their God" (Rev. 21:3).

God delights in being with His people, and He is pleased when His people are there for each other. Jesus indicated that this would be a measure of our success as His friends: time, attention, presence. Did you visit Me in prison? Clothe Me when I was naked? Feed Me when I was hungry? Did you come to the banquet when you were invited? Were your lamps oiled and ready for the Bridegroom's call? Did you put down your tasks to sit at My feet? Or did you always respond, "Let me go and do this first"?

To be there for my friend is to be Christlike, for Christ was literally "God with us," *Immanuel.* There is a cost involved in "being there." Jesus laid down His position, even His life, in order to be with us. I will have to lay down some of my benefits (leisure, rest, other relationships, personal goals) in order to be available for my friend. This is incarnation: Friend with me.

"I'll be there for you," says the theme song of a hit TV show. The message is clear; even the secular community recognizes it. A friend is there. To celebrate big moments, like the birth of your first child . . . and his graduation. In the crises. In life's transitions. For the fun and for the loss. For the conversation and the silence. A friend is someone like Millie, the neighbor from the sixties sitcom *The Dick Van Dyke Show*—someone who will run next door at a moment's notice. Or someone at the other end of the phone. Or at the other end of an e-mail.

Sheryl and I had only been friends for a few months before she and her husband and toddler were packing to return to the other side of the world, where they live and work. But we became fast friends when she was presented with the opportunity to adopt twins from a third world country. What a decision to make during an already hectic time. Up to her ears in packing crates, Sheryl e-mailed, "Pray." I did. I prayed with her for the next months. They were excruciating months, as Sheryl and Dan navigated a maze of a foreign government's red tape.

For several months, they camped out in small quarters in that place, showing up each day at one office or the other, only to be delayed again and again. Meanwhile, the twins became very ill, and the very awful possibility was presented that Sheryl and Dan might not be allowed to adopt them. My friend was also ill, plagued by a stomach parasite. She could not eat. She could not sleep. She could barely take care of her toddler. She was exhausted—physically, emotionally, spiritually. My heart ached for her.

Because we were on opposite sides of the world, her night was my day. I could cover her while she tried to sleep. But often in the midst of my day, I would start to e-mail Sheryl and find her on-line already, in the middle of her night, unable to sleep. I remember one particularly dark night for her.

Dear Karla, It is two A.M. *here, but I am tossing and turning. My heart is breaking. Today, we heard that the twins had been brought from the village where they were born. They are in terrible condition, particularly the little girl. She is malnourished and dehydrated. We think the woman who was caring for her was not using the milk she was given for the babies, but for herself. My sweet little girl had amulets tied around her wrists and ankles. Her caretaker does not worship the One we do, but had dedicated our baby to an idol. She will go into a hospital here, and we are not allowed to see her because we are foreigners. Please ask that the nurses will care for her. Please ask that she will be set free from the clutches of darkness. Please ask that she will live. —S*

Dear S, Oh my dear friend, how I hurt for you. When I think of you, I picture you holding back a wall of darkness that is threatening your little family—like the boy with his finger in the dike. You are exhausted from this. Please rest. Please let me hold back the darkness. I will take the night watch for you. Go to sleep, and know that someone else is standing guard. —KW

If I am to help my friend on her journey of faith, there will be times when I must say to her, as Christ said to His friends, "I will give you rest." There are many ways to say

"I will give you rest." "I will stand guard," is one way, as I did with Sheryl. I will pray when you have run out of prayers. I will sit by the phone or the bedside or in the hospital waiting room.

We also offer rest when we say, "I will take care of it." I will take your children for the afternoon. I will bring dinner. I will vacuum. I will make the phone calls. I will do the details, so you can close your eyes. A true friend does not say, "Let me know if I can do anything;" a true friend just does it. Because women are not good at asking; we're not going to let you know if you can do anything. We're just going to try to be strong.

I can offer you rest by not expecting you to be strong—in fact, by not expecting anything of you at all. My friendship can be to you a space free of expectation. There may be no other space like this in your life. What a relief to know there is someone who offers nothing but her presence: Come and sit on my porch. Have nothing to say. Be of no use. Do not be charming or even interesting. Just be here. You are welcome here. Jesus invites us, "Come as you are." That should be our invitation, too.

My home is not a quiet one, or even a very clean one most of the time! On a given day, there are six or seven boys of various ages over here, running in and out. My office is here, so I am usually working *and* doing laundry (for all those boys). So it surprised me when a friend who had just had her second miscarriage called me and asked, "Can I come over there and sit?" Of course I said she could, although I was a little nervous about whether she would be comfortable. She assured me she would.

My friend spent the whole afternoon at my house, curled up in an arm chair, reading magazines and staring out the window. I worked at my desk. I started dinner. I folded laundry. The kids played in the yard. We didn't talk. At the end of the afternoon when she left, she gave me a hug and said, "Thank you. I just needed a place to be sad."

A place to be—this is what God offers us. My friend Claire Cloninger has said that people should not be called human beings; we should be called "human do-ings" because that is how we define ourselves, by what we do. We were created as be-ings. The marvelous thing about heaven is that we won't have job descriptions. We will finally be what we were meant to be—be-ings. We will be with God, and that will be enough.

I need permission to do nothing. A friend can give it to me. In fact, I need a friend to do noth-ing with me! This is one of the great gifts of friendship—the gift of play. It's how we form our first friendships. Our mothers plop us down in the sandbox next to another girl, and we spend all afternoon digging together. We have tea parties. We kick soccer balls. We eat ice cream. Together we join hands and escape the world. When we grow up, we do not lose the need to play; we just lose the ability. Which is why we need friends who know how to play hard and play well. One definition that friends Ellen Goodman and Patricia O'Brien like describes play as "an up-side-downing of behavior." I remember hanging upside down on the monkey bars at the playground when I was a child. The sheer daring of it, dangling by your knees, feeling gravity pull in a new direction. The sheer silliness of it, your hair standing on end. We need to stand the world on its end from time to time. Play allows us to look at life from a new perspective—or not to look at it at all for a while. Play allows us to forget ourselves, which is really a great relief.

Our culture does not help us with this. Play has become a chore, a discipline. Just do it. We work at our play with a self-consciousness that constantly checks our pulse, measuring our progress. Those who play for a living—artists and athletes—play with such hubris that we, watching, learn to play for the audience, not for the joy. There is no "up-side-downing of behavior." The same rules of achievement/ drive/ competition/ success that we apply to work also apply to play.

Believers should understand "up-side-downing." We belong to an upside-down kingdom. Whoever is least shall be greatest. Whoever would be first should be last. Lose your life to find it. Jesus taught us that whoever would come into this kingdom would have to come as a child. Watch a child play. I used to love to do this when my children were little. Seth could spend hours in the back yard, lining up his stuffed animals, singing little songs to them, having private conversations. When a child plays, he is totally unaware of time and space. He loses himself. He is free.

I play with a group of friends who like to dig in the dirt. We call ourselves the Yard Angels. The Yard Angels work in the gardens and yards of each other, of other friends, of women who need a little help. We have worked in the gardens of women who were recently widowed or undergoing chemotherapy. We have planted gardens at Habitat for Humanity houses and helped a friend start a garden at her new home. We are a loosely formed group. You show up if you can and stay as long as you can. We start early in the morning and we always go to lunch after we're done. We go to lunch even though we are covered in dirt—and we are *covered* in it!

Yard Angels don't just weed and water. We dig. We shovel. We haul rocks. We trim trees and uproot bushes. All the while, we talk. We talk about our children, our grandchildren, our husbands, our houses. This is an added benefit of playing in the dirt together. As we sort out weeds, we also sort out complicated issues. When one of us admits that she probably should not squat in the dirt *and* laugh at the same time without wearing Depends, we all giggle—even as we breathe a sigh of relief at the recognition that yes, we are aging. Our bodies aren't doing what they once could. And it's okay, it's part of life, so laugh. We laugh a lot. We laugh at the sight of Peggy shinnying up a tree. We laugh at the sight of Lynne in short-shorts and goggles, revving her chain-saw. Once Brenda and I actually had a dirt-clod fight in the church flower bed. Always when it comes time to quit and go to lunch, we marvel, "Where did the time go?" That is a sure sign of authentic play. As my son Ben says, "Time flies when you're loving life!"

Play enables us to love life. It provides space for joy. It re-engages us in wonder.

The first time Vicki, Tami, Kim, and I went to the beach together, it was Vicki who took us. She had been to Kiawah Island many times before, and she wanted us to share it all with her—crabbing, shelling at low tide, riding bikes on the beach, shopping in Charleston. We went gladly, trusting the trip to her.

We arrived at one in the morning, found our way to our beach house, and stowed our bags and groceries. Then, handing us each a flashlight, Vicki insisted we follow her outside! Into the night we went, down winding paths, through thick pine woods, with no clue of where we were, like a troop of campers breaking curfew, with Vicki practically hopping up and down in excitement. Crossing over a boardwalk, we came to a sudden stop— and first we smelled it: the salt and the sea.

"Turn out your lights," Vicki whispered. We stood in the moonlight as the stars twinkled on the sand and the wind whipped around us. We could hear but not quite see the surf pounding beyond. In that moment, we were four girls again. Four girls on a sleep-over, counting the stars and wondering at the meaning of life.

Play is, after all, re-creation. God, the great Creator and Recreator, is constantly doing new things and surprising us with them. There is no telling where life will take you. Life has taken the four of us through many changes. We have not been to the beach in several years, but we plan to go this fall, and when we do, everything will be different. Life changes friends. The challenge for us is to let God re-create our friendship as He redesigns our lives. Cooperating with that process is not always easy.

I have another group of four friends; we call ourselves the Beloveds. I could tell you how that got started, but it's beside the point. The Beloveds were acquaintances, but we became heart friends when we bonded over a Bible study we did together. That was years ago. On one particular morning, we met for brunch to celebrate Mel's thirtieth birthday. The Beloveds are a fruit-basket of ages and life stages—thirties, forties, single, married, newly-wed, with children, without children, wanting children. We have each changed a great deal since we began together. Considering this group, I marvel that we are still friends. It takes effort because we are so diverse. It takes cooperation because all are so strong.

It is sometimes precarious to be friends with strong women. You all will have to learn to respect boundaries. You have to learn to allow give and take, solitude and togetherness, dependence and independence. These women were with me the day my husband was in a terrible car wreck. In my numbness, they thought for me, acted for me, saw to my children, saw that I ate, that I had clothes to wear. They sat with me and with Dennis. One evening in the hospital, Dennis whispered, "Honey, I'm cold," and three of us jumped up to get a blanket. Gigi laughed, "Which honey did you mean?"

On the other hand, there have been times when I profoundly wanted these women to butt out. I know Mel has felt that way. On the morning we met for brunch, Mel was about to make a huge transition in her life. She was leaving a highly respected profession for which she was highly trained. ("I know it's a dream job," she says. "It's just not my dream.") Mel was giving up salary, promotions, benefits, and the trappings of corporate success to go back to school and start over in ministry. At that moment, her best job prospect was camp counselor.

The Beloveds have alternately encouraged, prayed, prodded, scolded, and bullied Mel to follow her dream. We have offered to lend her our money, our spare bedrooms, our cars, our names on her resumé, and our husbands to do the heavy lifting. She was leaving us to take the first step on her journey: graduate school. We took her to brunch on her thirtieth birthday. Looking around that table filled with laughter, I knew things would not be the same. We would change, and so would our friendship. Mel was ready to go; she was looking ahead. And we had to let her go, because we were, in part, responsible. We were the ones who said, "You have what it takes. Go for it." Now we had to back up our words by letting go of her hands and sending her into her future.

Sometimes "being there" means not being there. A time to embrace, says Ecclesiastes 3, and a time to refrain from embracing. There is a time when being there means giving your friend space, giving her wings. This year I am taking my first son to college—which feels a bit like having my right arm ripped off. But it is time for me not to be the center of his world, not part of his daily life. I have been prepared for this moment by a lifetime of letting friends go, with the promise that I will always be there.

How can you and I be there for each other when we are not in the same stage of life? I may have to help you know how to be with me when my experience is not the same as your experience. I have learned this lesson from Nancy Guthrie. Nancy and Dave Guthrie have lost two children to Zellweger Syndrome, a rare metabolic disorder. When Hope, and then Gabriel, were born, Dave and Nancy had to go home from the hospital knowing the baby had only months to live. The Guthries not only faced this awful truth with remarkable faith; they also helped their friends to face it with them. When we didn't know what to say, they said, "Just tell us you don't know what to say. The worst thing to say is nothing at all, ignoring our pain. Just let us know that you love us and that you share our sorrow." The Guthries invited their friends to love Hope and Gabriel, but they also acknowledged how hard the process of caring for such a sick child was. When Hope and Gabriel died, Nancy and Dave provided practical ways of expressing grief.

After Hope died, I talked to Nancy about the day-to-day matters of returning to "normal" life. One of the things Nancy told me was that her friends with babies felt awkward, even guilty around her. They didn't know whether to include her in their activities because it might make her miss Hope.

"Of course I miss Hope," Nancy said. "But when mothers were willing to let it be awkward and to overcome the awkwardness by acknowleging it, then it didn't have to be uncomfortable for either of us anymore."

As your friend, I may have to willingly let you go on to a stage of life without me.

My friends Kim and Vicki trained with me for our prayerwalking trip. The terrain would be very mountainous, and we would be hiking, so we were getting our legs and lungs in shape.

One afternoon, we started up a steep hill. At that point in our training, Vicki and I were still unable to talk while simultaneously walking up this particular hill. We trudged along in companionable silence. Kim decided to run. I summoned up enough lungpower to shout, "Show off!" as she sprinted away.

Later I realized (I was not mature enough at the time) that I had just demonstrated why women tend to downplay their achievements around their friends. We are certain that in their hearts they are shouting, "Show-off!" We know how we feel when our friend becomes stronger, faster, surer than we are; we feel left behind. We feel like we felt in junior high when our best friend developed breasts before we did. But we *were* in junior high then; we aren't anymore.

What should I have yelled as my friend sprinted off up a hill I could barely climb? How about, "You go, girl!" I could have cheered her on, because I want her to be strong for the trip as much as I want it for myself.

Or do I?

What if my friend becomes healthier? What if she becomes wealthier, more confident, more educated, more experienced? What if she grows stronger in her walk with God and is able to run ahead up the path? What if I can't keep up? What if . . . she doesn't need me anymore?

The disciples expressed this fear to Jesus on the night He called them friends (see John 14). As He talked about what was coming, He could read the anxiety on their faces. "Don't let your hearts be troubled," He assured them. They couldn't go there yet, but they would join Him one day. Thomas said what they must all have been thinking: "Lord, we don't know where You are going, so how can we know the way?"

"I don't know where you are going!" is what I wanted to wail at Saralu when her "baby" graduated high school and moved to college, leaving Saralu and Ed to move into a new stage of life. Life with no kids, no boundaries on their free time. Suddenly they were going to movies— on weeknights! Saralu began to travel with Ed on his business trips. She was, well, a *real* grown-up. And I was not.

"There is no scriptwriter to help real women articulate the feelings of exclusion and loss," writes Ellen Goodman, "the fear that your best friend has just joined a new club from which you are barred." When you make cheerleader and I do not. When I get my first boyfriend and you do not. When the other girls on the hall get bids for sororities and no note is slipped under your door. When, as my friend Mel laughed, you have thirteen bridesmaid dresses in your closet, with shoes dyed to match—but no wedding dress. What happens when my friend gets married/ gets divorced/ gets pregnant/ gets a job—and becomes a different person? Is she still my friend?

Al and Tommye Shackleford and Lew and Vivian Reynolds were friends for over thirty-five years. Al and Lew were both in ministry. They worked together often. They raised daughters together. They met when the Reynolds moved to Indiana, where the Shacklefords already lived. Lew stayed with Al and Tommye when he first arrived.

"When we moved there to join him," Vivian recalls, "Tommye was the first person at my door." The four were inseparable from that day on. They spent every holiday together, went out every Friday night. Al and Lew's birthdays were two weeks apart; they were always celebrated together.

"Our girls even honored both men at Father's Day," Tommye remembers.

When the Shacklefords moved to Tennessee, the families remained fast friends.

"We burned up the road from Indiana to Tennessee!" they laugh. Holidays were still celebrated together.

"When Lew would go to Nashville for meetings, I would go with him," Vivian recalls. "He would stay in a hotel downtown, but I would stay with Tommye. Her church became my second church, like home to me. And we always sent each other cards. That is probably the second most important thing we have done for each other, next to spending time together."

Happily, the Reynolds moved to Nashville, and the four fell back into their routine. Tommye says she and Vivian became especially close, "Because that's what women do." The two look remarkably alike, with striking white hair, high cheekbones, and sparkling eyes.

"People ask us all the time if we are sisters," says Vivian. "Yes, we are, at heart. I think that's what they see more than the physical resemblance—the bond between the two of us."

"Our friendship is a gift God gave me," says Tommye. "We both look at it like that."

It's a friendship that has been through many transitions and one fiery test. On July 6, 2000, the Reynolds' fiftieth wedding anniversary, Lew had a massive heart attack. Three weeks later, the Shacklefords, coming home from a family reunion, were in a tragic head-on automobile collision. Tommye suffered serious injuries. Al was killed.

Vivian's voice becomes small and tearful when she talks about it. Her husband lived; Tommye's did not. How could anything be so unfair?

Some friendships might have faltered. Tommye and Vivian's did not. It has been forced by circumstances to change, both admit; but it has not lessened. Both women acknowledge the limits of friendship; husband and family come first. Both agree that's as it should be.

"Our friendship has a lot of mileage on it," Tommye says. "I've demanded a lot of Vivian, especially in the last few years. She has always been there for me. At times she dropped everything for me. When I had brain surgery, she washed my bald, shaved head. When I fell and broke my hip, she was at the rehab hospital day after day." Since Al died, Lew and Vivian have still kept Tommye company, bringing her to church, taking her out to dinner.

Just like a thirty-five year marriage, a life-long friendship has its ups and downs. There is a need for honesty. It takes commitment.

"Tommye gave me a music box that plays the song, 'You are the wind beneath my wings,'" Vivian recalls. "I have always taken that as my personal challenge—to be that for her whenever she needed it."

"I have lost friends," Virginia Woolf wrote. "Some by death—others through sheer inability to cross the street." Navigating the transitions of life requires a brave heart—one that will walk across the street to be with you, or just across the room, as happened to fourth grader Margaret Jane Staggs. Standing in the doorway on her first day in Sunday School, Margaret Jane had never felt so awkward. All the other girls were huddled in the corner of the room, whispering and laughing. Until Laura Ford, smiling, walked across to Margaret Jane and said, "Don't worry; we're not talking about you."

It never occurred to me, when Saralu's last child left home, that it was awkward for her as well. That she had to negotiate a relationship with her newly independent son. That she had to redefine her marriage after twenty years with children at home. That every time she went to the grocery store, she longed to buy the cart full of groceries it had once taken to feed her kids and their friends, that every time she opened the refrigerator door, the empty shelves were a reminder of the empty rooms upstairs. The change in our stages of life rocked my world; it never occurred to me how it must have stood hers on end.

Problems arise when we add friendship to that hope

chest which represents being settled: house, husband, family, career. Friendship is fluid when we realize it is the vehicle—the thing which carries us on our journey together—not the destination. We have not arrived when we have found a friend; we have just begun.

On our journey, we bring with us emotional baggage—the hurts, fears, expectations, and truths with which we have papered the walls of our hearts over a lifetime. This baggage affects our ability to adapt to change, our behavior in response to conflict, our capacity to give and receive love.

Kay and Becky worked together on a video presentation at work. Becky was the creative thinker, Kay the technical implementer. For days, they rehearsed their presentation until it was flawless. On the day of the actual presentation, one projector malfunctioned. The sequence of visuals was thrown off. As Becky stood wringing her hands, Kay deftly took apart the projector, identified the problem, fixed it, and caught up with the visuals in just the right place. As soon as the presentation ended, Becky threw her arms around her co-worker.

"Thank you!" Becky cried. Kay stiffened.

"I'm sorry I messed up," she said.

"Messed up?" laughed Becky. "You saved the day! I didn't have a clue what to do!"

Later, Kay stopped by Becky's desk. Awkwardly she said, "Hey, thanks for not yelling at me earlier when things went wrong."

That afternoon, Becky learned that Kay's father had been a stern man, impatient with incompetence, cold to Kay if she did not excel. At the crucial years of her adolescence, Kay's father left Kay and her mother. Kay always blamed herself for not being good enough to keep her father's love. She had brought that assumption to her friendship with Becky.

We expect to be loved as we have been loved, lavishly or pitifully. We impose this data on our relationship with God. If we have been rewarded for performance, we perform for God, fearing Him when we fail. If we have been inconsistently loved, we expect God to have the same mood swings. Here is where my friend steps in to play a crucial role. By being there, she proves that God will be there. Her faithfulness enables me to trust His faithfulness.

"My heart is not proud," begins King David in Psalm 131. "But I have stilled and quieted my soul; like a weaned child with its mother, like a weaned child is my soul within me."

The weaning of a child marks a stage in its growth. It marks its first venture into independence. The child can now eat many kinds of food and venture farther afield. It is growing up, but it is still a child and in no position to make any more than the simplest decisions, and those only under parental permission and guidance. And, at times, it has a nostalgic longing for the old closeness. The weaned child in Psalm 131 chooses—out of longing—to go back and lean against its mother. So we as friends must choose to allow ourselves to be loved. We must choose to lean on each other. Sometimes I worry I will wear out my friend with my needs. But in a lifelong journey, there will come a time when she will lean on me, and I will be there for her.

"Friendship is about reciprocal cherishing," write Elisabeth Young-Bruehl and Faith Bethelard in *Cherishment*. "It may come as a surprise that to be a good friend you might need to be able to receive loving care as well as give it. But this is the essence of friendship."

True friendship is, like marriage, a pledge to be there for better or worse, in sickness and health. When Paul urged his friends in Ephesus to "walk worthy of the calling," he went on to say, "Be completely humble and gentle; be patient, bearing with one another in love. Make every effort to keep the unity of the Spirit through the bond of peace." Unity is the goal so that we all grow up together. But unity isn't preserved because we're all nice people, or because we have no problems. Unity is preserved because we work hard at keeping it. We agree on this basic rule: no matter how our friendship changes or is tested, we are forever bound to each other through Christ and for Christ. Unity is preserved because Christ is Lord. It is our priority because Christ said it is His priority. Our ability to adapt and accept is proof that Christ is in us, a credential we offer to the world that Christ in a life does indeed make a difference.

We display this difference in the way we handle conflict: together—with honesty, prayer, and tenderness. Conflict in friendship is often a surprise to women. We expect tensions in our relationships with men, with parents, children, colleagues, but not with women friends. Therefore we are hesitant to address conflict, and sadly, many friendships end because of it. Either we distance ourselves, becoming too busy, failing to return phone calls or e-mails, or we nurture wounds that eventually blow up into angry fights.

It is proof to the world that Christ is Lord when we can overcome wounded feelings, angry words, hurtful actions, when we can adjust our expectations and accept each other's differences. We can do this solely if, in fact, Christ *is* Lord. I forgive you not because I may feel like it, but because I am commanded to forgive. You bear with me patiently in my immaturity not because it is easy, but because it is required. We may not be able to pray with each other or for each other until each has prayed a long time alone. The real conflict is not with each other; it is with our own selfish hearts, our own stubborn pride. We struggle to surrender our will to Christ's. We may not feel like giving in to each other, but we must give in to Christ. Despite our differences, this is what keeps us together: we both have Christ as Lord, and we both must struggle to obey Him.

I know two women, formerly best friends, who have survived a terrible betrayal: one had an affair with the other's husband. When it was discovered, it was heart-breaking, not just for them, but for all of us who loved them. We watched each of them deal with her shock, anger, grief, denial, despair. Wisely, they each went for solid biblical counsel and were told, "You must forgive." It was a long and wrenching process. I remember the first time they had to be in a room together. Every one of us held our breath. The grace with which these two wounded friends handled the moment was, as the old hymn says, amazing. They looked at each other through tearful eyes.

"This is hard for me," one whispered.

"Me, too," the other replied. "But I'm trying. And I'm not going to stop."

We display the difference that Christ makes in the way we handle adversity: together—with hope, patience, and confidence in God. "Whatever happens, conduct yourselves in a manner worthy of the gospel of Christ," Paul wrote to his friends in Philippi. "Then, whether I come and see you or only hear about you in my absence, I will know that you stand firm in one spirit, contending as one man for the faith of the gospel without being frightened in any way by those who oppose you" (Phil. 1:27–28).

"Contending as one man" means that every addition to my friend's life enriches mine, and every loss in her life diminishes mine as well. I will be there for her in both joy and sorrow, and in both, I want for her one thing: to know more of Christ and depend upon Him more fully. "Being there" does not make me her savior. In fact, when I try to save her, I keep her from knowing the One who is her Savior. As women, we often try to do too much for each other, instead of pointing out the need for Christ.

My friend Candi is a young woman in her mid-twenties. For two years, Candi served as a missionary to a country whose government is closed to the gospel. When Candi arrived on the field, her assignment was to be a student in a large city university. But an opportunity had just opened to place students at a small teaching college in a rural town that had never been open to foreigners before. No English-speaking person had ever lived there! No one in the village had ever heard the name Jesus Christ! Candi was offered the opportunity, and she took it. For four long weeks, she had no e-mail. We waited anxiously to hear from her. Finally, she wrote:

> I confess that since coming to the Last Frontier, my heart has become very hardened. I had convinced myself that I had to "be strong" or I wouldn't "cut it" here. The Father has shown me His invitation and promise in Psalm 50:15: "Call on me in the day of trouble; I will deliver you, and you will honor me." I am not a hassle or an inconvenience to Him! It honors Him when I call on Him! In the past month I have found myself clinging to this verse. Never before have I been so close to the front lines of battle.

With this greater awareness and dependence on our Father, my co-worker and I climbed into an over-packed van and marched out to conquer a new land. Obstacles were waiting for us the moment we arrived, namely the newly appointed "foreign affairs official," whom I have nicknamed "Darth Vader." Arrogant, greedy, and full of lies, Darth has made everything we'd already agreed upon—accommodations, rent, tuition and fees, government papers—a new fight. We face the daunting language barrier, as no one here, including Darth, speaks any English, and we have not yet mastered their language. By the third day, I acquired a cold. At 10,000 feet altitude, just breathing is difficult. My small one-bedroom apartment sometimes has electricity and running water. Above all, without phone lines for the past weeks, we basically had no form of outside communication, which felt something like being sucked into a black hole.

In this state of despair, the sovereign God of the universe met me. When I could turn to no one else, I turned to Him. And suddenly, I realized what He had done. For several years now, I have asked Him to take me to a place of total dependence on Him—and He has gone to great lengths to get me there!

How much He must love me!

It was Candi's last words which so profoundly convicted

me. If we who loved her could have rescued her, could have been the ones she turned to and listened to, would she ever have learned how much God loves her?

When Jesus began to tell the disciples what lay ahead for Him, Peter protested, "Never, Lord! This shall never happen to you!" Jesus turned and said to Peter, "Get behind me, Satan! You are a stumbling block to me; you do not have in mind the things of God, but the things of men" (Matt. 16:22–23). In Gethsemane, when the angry mobs appeared, Peter tried to protect Jesus again, and when he failed, Peter gave up in despair, finally denying that he even knew his friend.

What about you? Do you trust God enough to let your friend go through the trial? Do you trust God enough to wait in the darkness of the cross, the tomb—when hope has died? Do you trust that He is bringing about new life? Jesus did not need Peter to rescue Him. All Jesus required of Peter was that in the midst of the agony, Peter would be counted on to say, "Yes, I am with Him."

I cannot fix the fact that you have cancer. But I can be with you for the biopsy. I cannot fix the fact that your marriage is failing, or your job is ending, or your child is leaving. But I can be at your side, waiting with you in the circumstance.

Women wait together by doing. The manual tasks of baking, sweeping, stitching—these give us something to do when we cannot do anything about whatever is happening. They help us to wait. This is why women bring food, clean houses, sit by bedsides in times of crises. It is a constructive way of saying, "I am here with you in this."

When Al Shackleford died, I went straight around the corner to Tommye's house and headed to the kitchen. Elsie Graham was already there. We spent the next two days together, sweeping the floor, answering phones, taking messages, labeling casseroles, wiping countertops. There were no words to say. What had happened to Tommye was unspeakable. We could only be there. We could only wait with her through the long days.

This is the lesson we learn from Advent: how to wait. The season of Advent, the four weeks preceding Christmas, is that season in which we await the coming of Christ. In celebrating His birth, we also look forward to His return. December twenty-fifth was chosen as the time to celebrate Christ's birth because it was the European Winter Solstice, another celebration of anticipation—when during the darkest month of winter, the days begin their rotation toward spring, becoming longer and bringing with them the promise of light. For Christians, Advent is a busy time. Waiting involves preparation. Decorations are hung. Choirs are rehearsed. Food is prepared. Hearts are examined. Candles are lit. Gifts are made ready. All for the moment when the guests arrive, when everyone is gathered around the table, or the hearth, or the altar, and the Christ Child is welcomed into the world.

"Encourage each other with these words," Paul wrote

to his friends: "Our Lord is coming. And we will be with him forever" (see 1 Thess. 4:16–18). When time is no more—when there is no time—the most precious commodity will be presence. The presence of God and the presence of those who love Him, who love each other.

Most of Paul's friends outlived him. Had he not imparted to them the knowledge of Christ, they would have been left hopeless. None of us, no matter how much we love, can truly always be there. "No friend can be everything you need," Vivian Reynolds told me. Ultimately, the best way to be there for our friend is to point her to the One who will be with her forever. Take her by the hand and walk with her toward Him. Without Him, no matter how many friends she has, she is truly alone.

Chapter Four

Hold Me Accountable

Walk in all the way that the LORD your God has commanded you.
—Deuteronomy 5:33

I have tried to think of a fun story to begin this chapter on friendship. I couldn't think of one. I could only think of this quote by Marie von Ebner-Eschenbach: "There are very few honest friends—the demand is not particularly great." Quite frankly, this will be a difficult chapter. Accountability is not a fun aspect of friendship. But please don't skip it! Confrontation, confession, forgiveness, restoration . . . these are not easy acts, but if you can find a friend who will walk with you through them, you have found a jewel. Trust me, you will not trade her for a fistful of fun friends.

Come to think of it, some of my "funnest" friends are the ones who hold me most accountable for a holy lifestyle. I have giggled like a schoolgirl with Saralu Lunn. We have done crazy things together, thrown extravagant parties together. We have turned up the music loud and danced like teenagers. With this same friend I have hung my head in shame. I have wept tears over stupid blunders. We have prayed deep prayers together and read the Word to each other. She is the first one to look me square in the eye and say, "That is not worthy of you or God."

In *Life Together*, Dietrich Bonhoeffer wrote, "Where Christians live together the time must inevitably come when in some crisis one person will have to declare God's Word and will to another. It is inconceivable that the things that are of utmost importance to each individual should not be spoken by one to another. It is unchristian consciously to deprive another of the one decisive service we can render to him. Or do we really think there is a single person in this world who does not need either encouragement or admonition? Why, then, has God bestowed Christian brotherhood upon us?"

"I myself am convinced, my brothers, that you yourselves are full of goodness, complete in knowledge and competent to instruct one another," Paul wrote to his friends (Rom. 15:14). Or as another translation puts it, they are "able to admonish" one another. When Paul told his friends, "You are competent," or "able," he was using the Greek word meaning "empowered," empowered by *dunamis*—miraculous power, mighty working power, power which produces amazing results. Equipped with that power, we can admonish one another. *Admonish* is an old-fashioned word, a word that has been consigned to our religious vocabulary. It sounds frightening to admonish someone, but it simply means to gently reprove or call attention to.

"Jesus said to his disciples . . . 'So watch yourselves. If your brother sins, rebuke him, and if he repents, forgive him. If he sins against you seven times in a day, and seven times comes back to you and says, "I repent," forgive him.' The apostles said to the Lord, 'Increase our faith!' He replied, 'If you have faith as small as a mustard seed, you can say to this mulberry tree, "Be uprooted and planted in the sea," and it will obey you'" (Luke 17:1–6).

Dunamis—the power to uproot trees and throw them into the sea, just by our words. Jesus couples this with the gentleness and tenderness that repeatedly forgives. This is the environment in which accountability flourishes.

Accountability is simply giving each other permission to intrude. "Do two walk together unless they have agreed to do so?" (Amos 3:3) At some point in our friendship, I must say to you (and you must say to me), "I want you to call me on this. I want you to hold me to a standard," and that standard is God's Word. We must agree, you and I, that we want to walk together in obedience to

God, and therefore it is a mutual endeavor. We will be mutually accountable, mutually encouraging, mutually admonishing.

The basis for this accountability is our relationship to Christ. He is the head of the Body, and therefore the head of every relationship within the Body. "There is one body and one Spirit—just as you were called to one hope when you were called—one Lord, one faith, one baptism; one God and Father of all, who is over all and through all and in all," Paul explained (Eph. 4:4–6). Therefore, Paul concluded, we must "submit to one another out of reverence for Christ" (Eph. 5:21).

The community called the church exists because Christ loved the church and died for it (Acts 20:28, Eph. 5:25). The church functions because Christ empowered it (Matt. 16:18–20, 28:18–20; Acts 1:8). It is a result of His grace and under His authority. This is the foundation upon which every relationship within the community of Christ is built—husband and wife, parent and child, pastor and congregation, friend and friend. First and foremost, we belong to Him, and He is the head of us. That's where we must begin. There must be a mutual confession that Jesus is Lord, and therefore He is our authority. We consult His Word and obey it. We consider His will in our decisions. We make His priorities our priorities. We make His choice to love and forgive our choice to love and forgive.

This is the way we model His kingdom and His character to the world. We show it in our relationship to each other. We are a community that cannot be explained apart from the Spirit and our submission to His work in and among us. My pastor, Mike Glenn has said, "The confession that grounds the unity of the church is *Jesus is Lord*. The choice that determines our daily obedience is *Jesus is Lord*. The truth that affects our response to our circumstances is *Jesus is Lord*. That thing which sets us apart is *Jesus is Lord*. That thing which makes us dangerous is *Jesus is Lord*. That which ensures our victory is *Jesus is Lord*.

This was the key to the endurance of the New Testament church, in the face of intense persecution. It was the secret to the loving, unified community which won so much of the then-known world to Christ.

Two women who are believers must base all the actions of friendship upon their mutual agreement of the rule of faith. This is what Paul meant by the unity described in Ephesians 4. Not sameness—not even complete agreement on every issue. But complete agreement on one thing: Jesus is Lord. Therefore, we will obey Him. I will help you hold to that, and you will help me.

*H*olding each other accountable for holy living is not comfortable. It's a job we'd prefer to pass off to spiritual leaders, to those in authority—professionals. But when we professionalize the work of the priesthood, we nullify the work of Christ and the power of the Spirit. In ancient Israel, the work of interceding in prayer and offering forgiveness on the part of the people was delegated to the priestly line of Levi. However, God commissioned the entire community of Israel to be a "kingdom of priests" to the surrounding nations. The whole community was called to be obedient—so obedient that it was holy (set apart). This community would display God's character and authority to those nations that did not know Him (Ex. 19:3–6).

In between the Old and New Testament periods, the Pharisees became the religious experts. Jesus re-assigned the work to the people: You are salt. You are light. As Peter put it, echoing God's words to Israel, you are a royal priesthood. The biblical model, set by God and fulfilled by Christ, is that the community of believers call each other to account for their understanding and practice of spiritual matters, that we intercede for and administer forgiveness to one another. Why? Because we are a Body. If one of us is sick, the others are infected. If one of us is lame, the others are affected. If one of us falters, the progress of the whole body is impeded as we make our way toward the goal (remember the goal?): that all of us together be mature, fully like Christ. "We proclaim him, admonishing and teaching everyone with all wisdom, so that we may present everyone perfect in Christ," Paul wrote (Col. 1:28). In doing so, we present Christ to the world.

We have robbed the role of friendship by placing more value on spiritual gurus. As a result, we go to every

Bible study and spiritual conference available, but we are still very lonely in our pursuit of Jesus Christ. We are bewildered by these professional Christians, even as we admire them. How did they get that way? Where did they get that knowledge? We are impressed. But we do not get to see them struggle with the Word, sweat it out in their daily lives, arm-wrestle with God over the difficult parts. We don't see them work out their salvation.

Picture the Bible teacher who most impresses you. Recall one thing you learned from them which absolutely wowed you. Got that in your head? Now let me ask you this: How much more impact would those same words have if they came from the mouth of your friend? How much more weight would they carry if you had seen her sweat until she learned them firsthand?

"What we are looking for," my friend Esther Burroughs tells me, "is a woman with an underlined Bible." Yes. In fact, what we are looking for is a *friend* with an underlined Bible. What we need is someone who will walk with us in the daily stuff. This is what we are looking for when we plug a Christian tape into the car stereo. It's what we want from our pastors, and why we complain about them: they don't have enough time for us. Companionship on the way—this is what we long for. But companionship is not the role of a preacher, teacher, or Christian "professional." It is the role of a friend.

"This modern tendency to defer to the authority of experts, particularly in matters of soul, has to be resisted on all fronts. The Bible is first of all the people's book, not the professor's or the pastor's," Eugene Peterson writes. "My gut feeling is that the most mature and reliable Christian guidance and understanding comes out of the most immediate and local of settings. The ordinary way. We have to break this cultural habit of sending out for an expert every time we need some assistance. Wisdom is not a matter of expertise."

"The fear of the LORD is the beginning of wisdom," says the psalmist. "All who follow his precepts have good understanding" (Psalm 111:10). The Hebrew word for "understanding" is *sekel*. It means prudence, insight, discretion. Anyone—not just professional Christians, but anyone—who obeys God's Word is a person with the kind of insight, the kind of sense that can help me obey God's Word. That's the kind of friend I want walking beside me—someone with an obedient life. That's what I have to offer my friend, my own obedience and what I am learning from it. If I want to be that friend with the underlined Bible, I must actually open mine and study it— and put it into practice.

This is what I need help with: fleshing out what God intends for me in the context of real life, my life. My life consists of sweeping floors, washing endless trails of dirty athletic socks, driving and dropping off. How do I do this without resentment, without viewing it as drudgery? My life includes a career that places heavy demands on my time and energy. How do I succeed in my career, yet keep my soul intact? This is the battlefield of good and evil for me: Which movie may my pre-teen son go to see? Is Harry Potter okay to read? Should a Christian use a credit card? How nice a house is too nice, in God's opinion? What I need in a friend is someone who will say to me, "You don't need another pair of shoes" or "You didn't handle that conversation very kindly."

Are these unspiritual issues? I don't think so. Some of my best girlfriends are missionaries—how much more spiritual can you get? This is what we talk about: *My child pokes other children in the eye. I don't really like my boss. I'm having trouble sleeping. Am I a spiritual failure if I have to take depression medication? Do you know how long it takes to get around on a subway with two kids and a stroller? I never see my husband. I wish I had a husband. Do you think this guy could be my future husband? I don't think I'm doing a very good job at my job.*

This is what I need a friend to understand: behind every unspiritual topic of conversation, there is an urgent spiritual question. "All I do is laundry" really means, "I wonder if I'm making any difference in the world." So let's don't sort life into piles: this is sacred, this is secular. If you're my friend and you're a Christian, it's all the same thing. Let's start there.

I think women know that; in their hearts I think they get it. We just don't say it out loud. We go to church and we go to conferences and we listen to teachers on tape who talk about Isaiah and Romans, about transformation and repentance and dispensation. And we think, "Oh, my," and try our best to understand. Meanwhile, we go around assuming we're the only one who ponders the meaning of life while standing in front of the dryer. This makes us lonely, which is just where Satan wants a believer to be. He wants to isolate us, to get us to relegate God to religious issues only, to keep us from carrying God's Word into our days. Satan would love for us to be merely religious. The last thing he wants is two women sitting over lunch praying for God's wisdom.

Salvation must be worked out, like the apostle Paul said (Phil. 2:12). Theology is meaningless if it does not lead to discipleship. It's an intentional day-to-day choice to do it God's way at God's time. Those big theological words get worked out in what may seem like little non-ecclesiastical ways. Yet that daily walking together toward the goal, that is *ekklesia*—the Body of Christ. There is nothing more ecclesiastic than two women friends working out their salvation with fear and trembling.

Sometimes I am fearful. Sometimes I am weak and trembling. I thank God for my friends. Without the context of friendship, religion becomes simply a bunch of big words that are hard to understand. Living in community, the big words become realities. Here's what I mean: "Spiritual formation" is a phrase I see used in Christian tapes and books these days. I know it is something I need. But what is it, I wonder? How do I do it? It sounds like something for which I need a degree. Actually, spiritual formation is what God does in me, not something I do for Him. My role is getting out of the way and cooperating with God's work in transforming and conforming me to His likeness.

Well, of course I want to cooperate with that. My first inclination is to run right out and sign up for a Bible study on spiritual formation. And yes, that would probably be helpful. But what if . . . what if I opened up the Bible and read it for myself? What if I poured over it, asking God to talk to me about my life? What if I had a friend who knows me really well who would do that with me? What if, together, we considered our daily decisions in light of God's teaching? What if we discussed it, a lot? If we tried to see what God is doing and how to cooperate with Him? What if we called each other to say, "I had this thought" or "This is what I hear God saying"?

Wisdom comes when we try to find out what pleases God and we do it (Prov. 15:33, Eccl. 2:26). I love it when I get an e-mail or phone call from my friend Debbie Childers. Debbie loves God's Word, and nothing makes her more excited than figuring out how to apply it to life. She will take me from one end of the Bible to the other with breathless excitement. "God showed me the coolest thing today! Now follow this thought," Debbie will say as she leads me along by the hand, like a little girl leading her best friend to the best new secret place she has discovered.

God tells His secrets to those who fear Him, says

Psalm 25:14. Debbie Childers knows this. The women in my Sunday School class are discovering this as we pore over God's Word and discuss our lives in light of what it says. We started at the beginning of the Bible and decided to read through it chronologically. We crawled through the first five chapters of Genesis. (It took us five months!) Our goal is to understand God. Why does He act or not act? What does He think? What does He love? What does He hate? What does He require? Asking these simple questions has prompted an astonishingly enthusiastic response from God. He is delighted that we have asked. Let me tell you, it is as if we have unlocked a treasure box. (In fact, we have.)

"When I see my friend after a long time," Ralph Waldo Emerson wrote, "my first question is, Has anything become clear to you?" This is a good question for us to ask each other every day, even several times a day as we try to listen to God and obey. Accountability is really about being good listeners together. Paul commended his friends in Thessalonica "because, when you received the word of God, which you heard from us, you accepted it not as the word of men, but as it actually is, the word of God, which is at work in you who believe" (1 Thess. 2:13).

"This Biblical text of ours is the most accessible, most life-giving, most community-making book ever written. There is nothing quite like it," wrote Eugene Peterson, "[nothing like] what happens when a few Christians deliberately put themselves under its influence, prayerfully and obediently. It quite transcends matters of intelligence and sophistication. . . . One of the most perceptive Bible students I have ever been with was a truck driver who was nearly illiterate—but he had good ears. Oh, how he listened!"

Accountability is helping each other develop good ears with which to listen to God—at times, even being each other's ears. James 1:21 advises us how to listen: "humbly accept the word planted in you, which can save you." For believers, hearing is linked with obeying. God may have made something clear to me, but I have not really heard Him until I have also responded to Him by adjusting my life to what He has said. "Has anything become clear to you?" we ask each other. And the follow-up question is, "Are you doing it?" Because we don't always want to obey what we hear. "This is what the LORD says: 'Stand at the crossroads and look; ask for the ancient paths, ask where the good way is, and walk in it, and you will find rest for your souls.' But you said, 'We will not walk in it'" (Jer. 6:16).

Disobedience doesn't come as a shock to God. Man's been doing it ever since we were created. But it is a sticking point with God. Obedience is a line He draws in the sand. He absolutely requires it, and therefore we must require it of each other. Why? Primarily because God deserves it. Period. But also because obedience is an indication of the condition of the listener's heart.

In Mark 4:1–20, Jesus tells His disciples the parable of the sower and the seed, which teaches us a lesson about God's Word and how it is received by its hearer. Like the soil that received the seed in the parable, every human heart contains some trampled soil, some areas where our lives are so heavily trafficked there is no space for the Word of God to take root. Every heart contains some rocky soil, some bits of us that are so shallow and immature that God's Word has no firm hold, where we are inconsistent and easily swayed. And every heart has its thorny patches too full of its own lists of concerns to even consider God's agenda. God is at work in us to till up some of that poor ground, converting it into a healthy medium in which the life of the Spirit can take root and flourish. He does this through Scripture, through prayer and meditation, through the Holy Spirit who convicts us, persuades us, teaches us. And He also does it through a faithful believing friend.

"It is one of the severest tests of friendship to tell your friend of his faults," Henry Ward Beecher wrote. "To speak painful truth through loving words—that is friendship." I will be called upon to confront my friend at times. I will have to say, "Look, this is not right" or "This has no place in your life." This might be extremely uncomfortable for me. But what do I want more—my comfort? Her comfort? Or her true best: maturity in Christ? I can choose whether I want my friend to like me or to be like Christ. A serene relationship is not necessarily a saving relationship. Christlike love isn't always serene.

To not speak God's Word to a friend is to be an enabler, to let her go on being sick, to leave her a prisoner to whatever holds her. Bonhoeffer wrote, "Sin demands to have a man by himself. It withdraws him from the community. The more isolated a person is, the more destructive will be the power of sin over him. . . . Sin wants to remain unknown. It shuns the light. In the darkness of the unexpressed it poisons the whole being of a person. This can happen even in the midst of a pious community. . . . The unexpressed must be openly spoken and acknowledged. All that is secret and hidden is made manifest. It is a hard struggle until the sin is openly admitted. But God breaks gates of brass and bars of iron (Isaiah 45:2)."

"I will break down gates of bronze and cut through bars of iron," God said in Isaiah 45:2–3. "I will give you the treasures of darkness, riches stored in secret places." Those treasures held in darkness may be our friends, bound by the chains of shame and secret sin. James wrote, "Therefore confess your sins to each other and pray for each other so that you may be healed" (James 5:16).

"The greatest psychological insight, ability, and experience cannot grasp this one thing: what sin is," wrote Bonhoeffer. "Worldly wisdom knows what distress and weakness and failure are, but it does not know the godlessness of men. And so it also does not know that man is destroyed only by his sin and can be healed only by forgiveness. Only the Christian knows this. In the presence of a psychiatrist I can only be a sick man; in the presence of a Christian brother I can dare to be a sinner."

It does take daring to confess sin to a friend, to put a name on that ugly thing in your life, to acknowledge it. You shatter your carefully constructed image of yourself. You get a new glimpse of who you are, and it is not a pretty sight. Worse, your friend sees it, too. Surely she will shrink in horror. Better to be vague, you think. Just be general. "I'm dealing with some issues," you say. "Pray for me." The last thing we want to be is a woman "caught in the act."

The woman caught in adultery and brought before Jesus walked away knowing the specific sin for which she had been forgiven (John 8:3–12). She walked away knowing exactly what Christ required of her. "Go now and leave your life of sin." Precisely for this reason, we must shine the light of confession on specific sins, so that we have specific healing.

When Christ shines His light on my particular sins, He deals with me about the areas of excess in my life. There are areas in which I am undisciplined and indulgent—issues like eating and owning stuff and overbooking my calendar. When I first began to be seriously convicted about my undisciplined eating, the weight of it caused me to come unglued in front of a dear friend. She responded in the way any loving friend would.

"But Karla," she said, "you are so funny and smart.

Everybody loves you just the way you are. You don't have to be perfect."

True, but I knew I had to be obedient. And I knew this was the area in which God was requiring it.

"This is serious," I told my friend. Just to make sure she understood how serious, I told her something I have never told anyone. I told her how much I weighed. I told my skinny friend my weight, which was almost twice hers. She tried very hard to keep her face still and composed. I thought she might faint. Her eyes got big. And then they filled with tears. She laid her thin hand on my fat arm.

"Oh, honey," she said softly. "We have the same problem. There isn't a moment that goes by that I don't obsess about food. I just obsess about not eating. You obsess about eating. We're both consumed by it. I know just how to pray for you."

Truly, it was a relief to be a sinner in front of my friend. Yes! Someone understood! But as Ellen Goodman and Patricia O'Brien wrote, there are times when a friend must provide more than the "warm soup of empathy." She must become a catalyst for change. Believers are called upon not only to confess our sin but also to correct it.

"He who hates correction is stupid," says Proverbs 12:1. The word *stupid* in this verse comes from a Hebrew word for animal or beast. If you hate correction, you are basically dumb as an ox. Stubborn as a mule. You're not going to grow, spiritually speaking. You're going to stay rooted right where you are, in your current predicament, being led around by whatever carrot is dangling in front of your nose.

According to the apostle Paul, all Scripture, because it is God-breathed, is useful to a Christian who wants to grow in righteousness. Paul identified ways in which the Scripture can be useful:

To teach a spiritual truth.

To rebuke: convict me of the way in which I fall short of this truth.

To correct: show me the action I need to take to get back on track.

To train me to stay on that course with endurance—spiritual muscle.

I can't just know the truth, or even simply confess where I fall short. The process is not complete unless I follow through with actions that correct my disobedience, with training that develops the ability to keep going once I have determined the course. In all these stages, I need my friend to hold me accountable. "As iron sharpens iron, so one man sharpens another," says Proverbs 27:17. But you can't sharpen iron against iron without some sparks flying. There is bound to be tension, even anger, in an accountable friendship. There will be times when I don't want to hear the truth, nor be held to it. What is a friend to do?

First, a friend should **be compassionate** because God

is compassionate. He demonstrated His love for us through Christ even while we were still disobeying (Rom. 5:8). Remember, He does not demand obedience so that we will be good enough, but because He is concerned with the state of our hearts.

"The basis upon which Christians can speak to one another is that each knows the other as a sinner, who, with all his human dignity, is lonely and lost if he is not given help," wrote Bonhoeffer. "We speak to one another on the basis of the help we both need. We are gentle and we are severe with one another, for we know both God's kindness and God's severity." I can be compassionate with you when you are acting immaturely because I am aware of the shallow soil in my own heart. "Be completely humble and gentle," Paul wrote. "Be patient, bearing with one another in love" (Eph. 4:2). "Forgive as the Lord forgave you" (Col. 3:13).

Second, **be discerning**. "The purposes of a man's heart are deep waters, but a man of understanding draws them out" (Prov. 20:5). There's that word *understanding* again—*sekel*. Insight. Discretion. Knowing the appropriate thing to do at that moment. If I am in the middle of a battle with God, the last thing I need from you is a lecture from the sidelines. I am not listening to God; what on earth makes you think I will listen to you? When I am unwise, I need you to be wise. Be quiet. Listen *for* me, because I'm not listening at the moment. And listen *to* me. Ask a lot of questions.

"When you respond, use clarifying questions and empathetic statements that reflect what you've heard her say," advises author Ann Hibbard. "As you identify the emotions your friend is experiencing, she will feel understood and will share further. This kind of active listening will help both of you to discern what's going on in her heart."

Jesus was this kind of discerning listener. He asked lots of questions. Look at His conversation with Nicodemus in John 3. Nicodemus came under the pretext of arguing Christ's authority. Imagine him nervously sitting across from Jesus, twisting the fringe of his shawl, looking over his shoulder. And Jesus, quietly and calmly bringing forth the real issue. *Why have you come under cover of night, Nicodemus? What do you really want to know? Aren't you a teacher of the Scriptures? Don't you already know what you need to know in order to believe? Or is there something else, something outside your control that's bothering you?*

That's what I need, a friend who will help me figure out, "Hey, what's really bothering you about this thing? What is it that frightens you so much you can't step out and follow God? Is it that you won't succeed? Or that you can't be in control? Or that you don't have all the answers?" And please, please don't give me the answers, even if you have them, even if I ask for them. Your role is to go with me to the source of all answers, the source of the faith to obey without answers. Take me by the hand,

and let's go together to God. In fact, if I ever come to you in my confusion and the first thing out of your mouth is, "Well, *I* think . . .," then I should definitely not listen to you. I do not need to know what you think; I desperately need to know what God thinks. "A fool finds no pleasure in understanding but delights in airing his own opinions," says Proverbs 18:2. Oh, how I need a friend who finds pleasure in understanding.

Try to discern the source of your friend's disobedience. Sometimes a friend's behavior is a result of wrong or incomplete understanding of Scripture. Consider Acts 18:24–26: "Meanwhile a Jew named Apollos, a native of Alexandria, came to Ephesus. He was a learned man, with a thorough knowledge of the Scriptures. He had been instructed in the way of the Lord, and he spoke with great fervor and taught about Jesus accurately, though he knew only the baptism of John. He began to speak boldly in the synagogue. When Priscilla and Aquila heard him, they invited him to their home and explained to him the way of God more adequately."

Aquila and Priscilla were not scholars or theologians. They had not been privileged to study in Jerusalem, as Paul had been. They were tentmakers. But they took their new faith seriously, learning and living out its doctrine. When they recognized that Apollos's understanding fell short, they were conscientious to gently instruct him in what he did not know. Priscilla and Aquila wanted Apollos to mature in his understanding and obedience.

Apollos only understood the baptism of John: repentance. He did not know the grace of Christ. Here's why we admonish one another—so that our friend will know the full benefits of life in Christ.

Paul wrote in Romans 15 that the Scriptures were written to teach us, so that through endurance and the encouragement of the Scriptures we might have hope. "May the God of hope fill you with all joy and peace as you trust in him, so that you may overflow with hope by the power of the Holy Spirit" (Rom. 15:13). We want our friend to understand the Scriptures so that she will have endurance and encouragement. Life is hard, and if we do not know the promises and truths of God, we lack the power to face it.

Perhaps Apollos received this new piece of truth joyfully, because it furthered his faith. But maybe your friend won't. Paul counseled Timothy to speak the Word "in season and out of season." Not all Scripture will be well-received. Ask yourself why. Is it the spirit in which you delivered it? Is it the timing? Is it the state of your friend's heart? Is it too frightening, too painful? Is her faith too immature? Does she need time to accept and obey this lesson? Or is she just willfully disobedient? This is an important distinction to make: Is my friend's behavior a continual, repeated disobedience to what she knows is correct?

The story of Noah is in the book of Genesis. It begins with a God's-eye view of the state of mankind—this kind of repeated, intentional disobedience. "The LORD saw how great man's wickedness on the earth had become, and that every inclination of the thoughts of his heart was only evil all the time. The LORD was grieved that he had made man on the earth, and his heart was filled with pain. So the LORD said, "I will wipe mankind, whom I have created, from the face of the earth—men and animals, and creatures that move along the ground, and birds of the air—for I am grieved that I have made them" (Gen. 6:5–7).

God saw that the intent and thought of mankind was *continually* evil, and it grieved Him. What is my appropriate response to my friend's behavior when she continually refuses to obey God and chooses destructive, even evil options? I don't get to wipe her out, because I'm not God. But I can grieve for her, because God does. Grieve for the death of her relationship with Him—by her own deliberate choice. "'There is no peace,' says the LORD, 'for the wicked'" (Isa. 48:22). That word *wicked* means willfully disobedient. Grieve for your friend, who will have no peace until she obeys God. Grieve for her ultimate judgment—separation. Pray for her.

"Blessed are those who mourn," Jesus said (Matt. 5:4). Blessed are they who grieve over sin and its consequences. Your friend will have to suffer the consequences of her disobedience. This hurts her, and you hurt for her.

What you want for your friend is reconciliation. You want her relationship with God restored. That's precisely what God wants, so take the same approach He does.

Third, **offer her love.** "Who is like the LORD our God, the One who sits enthroned on high, who stoops down to look on the heavens and the earth? He raises the poor from the dust and lifts the needy from the ash heap," says Psalm 113:5–7.

God "does not treat us as our sins deserve," says the psalmist. "For he knows how we are formed, he remembers that we are dust" (Psalm 103:10, 14). When I sin, God looks at me and recalls that moment in Eden, facing a disobedient Adam. He remembers forming us from the dust of the ground. He remembers pronouncing the consequence of Adam's sin: from dust you are, to dust you will return. Yes, we are Spirit, for Christ lives in us, but we are essentially earthly. We are of this dust, and its gravity holds us, not just by physics, but by human nature.

"May those who delight in my vindication shout for joy and gladness," says Psalm 35:27. "May they always say, 'The LORD be exalted, who delights in the well-being of his servant.'" A friend who walks worthy is one who shares God's delight in the well-being of His servant. She works to restore that well-being.

I want for my friend what Paul described when he wrote to his own friends: I want God to strengthen her inner being, fill her heart with faith. I want her to be rooted, established, firmly grounded in love. I want her to be able to grasp how wide and long and high and deep is the love of Christ and to know this love by personal experience—so that she may be filled to the brim with Christ (Eph. 3:16–19). The power of accountability has its rootedness in love. The one who holds the standard must love, and the one who struggles to attain it must know she is loved.

Fourth, **offer her truth.** "Reckless words pierce like a sword, but the tongue of the wise brings healing" (Prov. 12:18). When your time comes to speak, do so very carefully. Do your best, as Paul counseled Timothy, to be a workman who correctly handles the Word of truth (2 Tim. 2:15). Be careful of wielding Scripture carelessly or bending it to make a point. The Word of God is a scalpel (Heb. 4:12)—dangerous when not in the hand of a skilled surgeon trained to use it precisely and purposefully, for healing not wounding.

Be afraid—be very afraid—of saying anything "for her own good." Rarely does her good truly come out of what is said in that spirit.

Ginger was the coolest girl in my sixth grade. She and her best friend Shelly ruled the playground. Ginger lived right behind me. I was the new girl, and I wanted to be her friend so badly.

Just across the street from our elementary school was a corner drugstore, the kind with an old soda fountain. For a nickel, you could get one of those tiny Coca-Cola glasses filled with Cherry Coke. Every day when we would walk home from school, the kids would stop at the drug store. And Ginger and Shelly would take me over in the cotton ball aisle to explain to me whatever dumb or un-cool thing I had done that day—for my own good. Ever since then, I get a sinking feeling in my stomach when someone says, "I need to talk to you." I may be a grown-up, but once again, I'm standing in the cotton ball aisle.

There must be a Ginger and a Shelly in every sixth grade, because my friend Cindy had a similar experience. Although we laugh about it, she understands how much that memory hurts. One day she showed up at my door with a gift: a package of those cotton rounds you use to remove cosmetics. Attached to the package was a note which read, "No more cotton balls."

Matthew 12:36 tells us that we will be called to account to God for every careless word we have spoken. As your friend, I will be called upon by God to speak His Word to you. I must be very sure that I speak only His Word, His way, in His timing. Jesus Himself was very careful about this. He spoke bluntly, sometimes harshly. "I do nothing on my own," Jesus said, "but speak just what the Father has taught me" (John 8:28). This is exactly how careful I must be when speaking truth to my friend.

Fifth, **offer her freedom**. I cannot say this any more clearly than Dietrich Bonhoeffer did in his book *Life Together:*

> Because Christ has long since acted decisively for
> my brother, before I could begin to act, I must
> leave him his freedom to be Christ's; I must meet

him only as the person that he already is in Christ's eyes.

[Spiritual love] will rather meet the other person with the clear Word of God and be ready to leave him alone with this Word for a long time, willing to release him again in order that Christ may deal with him. It will respect the line that has been drawn between him and us by Christ, and it will find full fellowship with him in the Christ who alone binds us together. This spiritual love will speak to Christ about a brother more than to a brother about Christ. It knows that the most direct way to others is always through prayer to Christ and that love of others is wholly dependent upon the truth in Christ.

God did not make this person as I would have made him. He did not give him to me as a brother for me to dominate and control, but in order that I might find above him the Creator. . . . God does not will that I should fashion the other person according to the image that seems good to me, that is, in my own image; rather in his very freedom from me, God made this person in His image. I can never know beforehand how God's image should appear in others.

As Ann Hibbard says, Jesus simply told the truth and gave the other person the liberty to make the choice.

Finally, **be faithful to and be consistently patient with your friend while she struggles to obey.** Place your life alongside her. Walk with her—at her pace. Observe what is hindering her from "running the good race." You can leave her in your spiritual dust as you walk on ahead, but you will miss the opportunities that come by being alongside. These opportunities are the entry point for which God is watching. And you must watch, too. Watch carefully as the circumstances shift and the Spirit works, applying pressure, quickening the heart, bringing your friend to the point at which she is ready to hear and obey. God is the master of the art of timing. Go along. He has called you into this friendship not to run ahead of Him, not to get bored when the process is slow, not to lag behind when the work is difficult.

If we are faithful, we will get better at this with time. We will experience the relief of confessing, asking for help, accepting correction. We will enjoy each other's victories enough to pursue more of them together. And this becomes worth the risk. "So those who love must try to act as if they had a great work to accomplish," wrote the poet Rainer Marie Rilke. We do.

Chapter Five

Encourage Me in the Spirit

*If you've gotten anything at all
out of following Christ . . .
be deep-spirited friends.*
—Philippians 2:1–2 The Message

My Sunday school class has been studying the book of Job. One week, we read chapter 3 in which Job, having been afflicted with all sorts of unexpected disaster, sits on his ash heap and cries, "Why? Why? Why?" As we began to talk about the unexplained whys of our lives, I noticed tears silently running down Malinda's face. Malinda had been struggling along for months in a job that made her absolutely miserable. She had—we all had together—

asked God many questions. Malinda wanted to know: "Why am I in this job? Is there a reason You have me here? Is there somewhere else I should be? Am I supposed to be looking for the next thing or being faithful in this thing?" After all those months, her biggest question was, "Why are You not answering me?" That Sunday, we stopped our class in mid-discussion, and we all put our hands on Malinda and prayed. We asked God to give her an answer—any answer—just some part of the answer, so that she would know how to be faithful.

The next Sunday morning, we were chatting and drinking coffee as we waited for everyone to gather. Malinda came in bearing donuts.

"Well, I have news," she said, joining our circle.

We were all anxious to hear what had happened.

"I got fired on Friday!"

There was a moment of stunned silence, and then— we all burst into laughter, including Malinda! Melanie entered at that moment. "What?" she said, and we told her. Melanie, too, cracked up. We were all laughing hysterically, except Becky, who wasn't present the week before and clearly thought we had lost our minds.

"We prayed for Malinda's job last week," Joanne said to Becky between gasps of laughter. "Would you like us to pray for *you?*"

A funeral director once told me, "Only Christians laugh at funerals." Only Christians laugh at being laid off. Only Christians look expectantly at the unexpected, stand on the precipice and prepare to jump. Malinda told us that when her boss broke the news, she had to stop herself from grinning. Her boss was annoyed because she wasn't upset.

Around the room, the women nodded their heads. Yes, we understand this strange behavior. We appreciate the gravity of Malinda's situation. She doesn't yet have all the answers. But we know God, and we know that He does. We didn't ask Him for all the answers—just one. And He gave it. As Melanie said it, "That is *so* God!"

In Paul's letter to his friends in Ephesus, before he challenged his friends to "walk worthy of the calling"— before he discussed the nuts and bolts of this lifestyle— Paul painted for them a picture of the wild, free, limitless life into which they had now been born.

It's in Christ that we find out who we are and what we are living for. Long before we first heard of Christ and got our hopes up, he had his eye on us, had designs on us for glorious living, part of the overall purpose he is working out in everything and everyone.

It's in Christ that you, once you heard the truth and believed it . . . found your-selves home free—signed, sealed, and deliv-ered by the Holy Spirit. This signet from God is the first installment on what's com-ing, a reminder that we'll get everything God

has planned for us, a praising and glorious
life.

That's why . . . I ask—ask the God of
our Master, Jesus Christ, the God of glory—
to make you intelligent and discerning in
knowing him personally, your eyes focused
and clear, so that you can see exactly what it
is he is calling you to do, grasp the immen-
sity of this glorious way of life he has for
Christians, oh, the utter extravagance of his
work in us who trust him—endless energy,
boundless strength!
—Ephesians 1:11–19 *The Message*

Paul went on to make an astounding statement: This
energy and strength at work in us is *the same energy and
strength* God exerted when He raised Christ from the
dead and seated Him on the throne in heaven! That is
the power at work in and around you and me in what appear to be normal lives. In Christ our lives are anything
but normal. One of the most important things we can do
for our friend is to help her recognize this. Paul always
coupled a discourse on "how to walk" with a reminder:
This is who you are, and this is Who you walk with. So
expect amazing, mysterious things out of life. Welcome
the unexpected. One of the distinguishing marks of the
Christian community is the supernatural activity among
us: forgiveness, restoration, leaps of faith, provision,

healing, joy—those things which cannot be explained apart from the presence and action of God. That is the life of the Spirit.

The Spirit convicts us of our need for God (John 16:8).

The Spirit is the proof that we have received the life of God (Romans 8:14, 1 John 3:24).

The Spirit reveals to us the deep things of God (1 Corinthians 2:10–14, John 15:26).

The Spirit calls and appoints on behalf of God (Acts 13:2–4, Luke 4:16–21).

The Spirit empowers us to speak for God (Acts 1:8, Mark 13:11, Acts 4:31).

The Spirit enables us to know and obey God (John 14:26, Ezekiel 36:26–27).

The Spirit leads us as we follow God (Psalm 143:10, Isaiah 30:21).

The Spirit makes it possible to pray to God (Ephesians 6:18, Romans 8:26–27).

The Spirit gifts us with abilities to do the work of God (1 Corinthians 12:4–11, Exodus 31:1–6).

"Since we have this kind of life by the Spirit," Paul wrote, "let's keep in step with the Spirit" (Gal. 5:25, paraphrase mine). Keeping in step with the Spirit might mean taking baby steps, or moving at a crawl, or even sitting still. It often requires long stretches of daily doggedly putting one foot in the front of the other. At times, it will also mean running to keep up, leaping off cliffs, learning to fly.

"This is the landscape of faith," wrote author Sharon Salzberg in her book *Faith*. "Those things that bring us to our edge lead us to the heart of the mystery of life." It is precisely when I come to my own edge that I need to hold the hand of a friend as I step into the mystery of life. It may be the moment when I must admit I am not in control of events, when life takes itself back into its own hands. It may be that moment when I face the fact that I can't keep up, when I admit to weakness, when I bend over doubled, out of breath and out of stamina. Or when I am shaking with fear. That is when I need a deep-spirited friend, one who understands that the road of mystery is navigated by prayer, who knows the landscape of faith, which is the dwelling place of the Spirit.

I was in Dallas once for a weekend with a group of women at a hotel. After the retreat was over, I had arranged to meet a new friend, Charlotte, for lunch. Although Charlotte lives in another country, she was in Dallas for a few months. When we found we were to be in the same city, we arranged to meet.

At the retreat, to my surprise, my dear friend from college, Tammy, was there. Whenever I am in Dallas, I try to get together with Tammy and our other college pal,

Suzie. Guess what? The only time we could manage was lunch on Saturday, when I had planned to meet Charlotte. So there I sat in the hotel restaurant with a hodgepodge of women friends: Charlotte, accompanied by her daughter Holly; Tammy and Suzie, whom I hadn't seen in at least a year, and my hostess from the retreat, another Tammy. I expected it to be an awkward group, mostly chit-chat, which I hate. But I should know better about both God and women.

We talked about my recent visit to Charlotte's corner of the world, and Charlotte said to my hostess, "You should come!" Tammy replied, "I can't go anywhere right now. My father has Alzheimer's, and I'm his caregiver. But someday." And then she became teary and whispered, "Oh, that's awful. If someday I can go, that will be because my dad is gone."

Suddenly we were no longer strangers. We were all just, well, women. Women with lives, with families. Charlotte was in Dallas for a few months because her own sister was in the final stages of cancer. It was hard for her to be there, torn between wanting to make important contacts for her work but not knowing how long she had with her sister. I knew that while I was working there that day, I was missing my son's play-off game. It's hard to be a woman, because it's hard to give yourself away in pieces, as life demands a woman do. Only another woman can really know this. It is why we need each other. It is why we can and should pray for each other.

We think it is such a small thing to pray, and it is; it is a small thing when viewed as part of the whole scope of activities in the world yesterday or today. A handful of people bent to the business of an unseen kingdom—merely a handful, because not all Christians pray, certainly not for anything but themselves, and then Christians are such a small minority of the world's people. So we think our prayers are small business.

But just now, as I was writing, I was interrupted to go around to the side of the house—we have a woodpecker working on the porch!—and I noticed the ground is covered with acorns. Small kernels, with their little hats. I used to collect them at my great-grandmother's farm, under the big tree out front, and make tea cups of them for my dolls. Such small things. I gathered a handful of acorns and, bringing them back to my seat here, got a glimpse of the world from God's viewpoint. A small acorn becomes a mighty tree. A small act of faith, a prayer, becomes the movement of God's hand in some part of the kingdom. We live by these small/big things which are unseen. My handful of acorns sits here on my table, a reminder of the handful of prayers gathered today by my God. Small acts of faith in a faithless world. So I will go on, must go on, praying. "More things are wrought by prayer than this world dreams of," wrote Alfred, Lord Tennyson.

Ecclesiastes 11:1–6 says, "Cast your bread upon the waters, for after many days you will find it again. Give portions to seven, yes to eight, for you do not know what disaster may come upon the land. If clouds are full of water, they pour rain upon the earth. Whether a tree falls to the south or to the north, in the place where it falls, there will it lie. Whoever watches the wind will not plant; whoever looks at the clouds will not reap. As you do not know the path of the wind, or how the body is formed in a mother's womb, so you cannot understand the work of God, the Maker of all things. Sow your seed in the morning, and at evening let not your hands be idle, for you do not know which will succeed, whether this or that, or whether both will do equally well."

When writer Alexandra Johnson was a girl, she thought the change her father emptied from his pockets each night onto his bureau was what he earned that day. We take our ordinary concerns to God in prayer. We empty the day's change onto our Father's bureau. It seems so small an amount to contribute. That's because we mistakenly assume it is all the evidence of what He did today. But if you've ever emptied day after day of pocket change into one container, you know that it accumulates into a nest egg. We have no idea how our Father is investing our pocket change, putting our daily prayers to work. We are called to be faithful to daily empty our pockets onto His bureau.

In my Friday morning Bible study, I tell the women about the friends I have met on mission trips, particularly those in areas closed to the gospel. I pass around an envelope full of scraps of paper on which are handwritten requests by these women so far away. I pass them around with all the excitement of a child who has an object for "Show and Tell."

Karole Harrell asks if she can keep a particular one. I say, "Yes, but only if you promise you really *will* pray for her faithfully."

On Sunday morning, Karole, husband in tow, finds me and says, "I just want you to know I *am* praying for this woman, and I pray the same things for my own life, too."

This is how we pray for each other—we pray the same things we pray for our own lives, too. Anne Frame said to me as she looked through the handwritten notes, "What strikes me about these is that they're so *normal*." This is what strikes me about prayer: it is so normal. We make such a big deal of it, so it becomes difficult. But prayer is not a big deal because of anything we do; what is big is what God does. Prayer is nothing more than talking with God about normal things. God loves normal things. In normal things, God does His best work. God works with the common to produce the uncommon. When will we get the hang of that?

These are some of the requests my missionary friends have sent home with me:

"I wish my friends from home would be able to understand why God has me here."

"I'm lonely. There's no one here my age. I don't really relate to my coworker. I wish I had just one friend."

"I'm having a hard time raising three children with a husband who travels a lot."

"Pray for me. I'm losing weight, and I don't know why. My doctor doesn't either. It's becoming a health issue, and I don't want it to keep me from staying here."

"I will pray for you," usually means, "I will think of you fondly every now and then." The hard work of prayer is waiting alongside the other, persevering in asking, listening for answers, and telling each other what you hear. It is helping your friend adjust to the answer she may not expect or want. It is learning about God, His thoughts, and His ways. It's constantly acknowledging Who is in charge and leading your friend back to Him.

From my friends around the world, I have learned the importance of *asking* in prayer. My friend Mollie and her team cannot use religious words like *prayer* and *God* in conversation where they live. Instead, they *ask*, which I think is a better term for us humans to use anyway. I have been with Mollie when an unexpected turn of events threw all our plans up in the air. While I was standing there wracking my brain for solutions, I looked at Mollie, who was quietly whispering, "Father, I am asking . . ." Mollie and her team stop at every turn and ask, "Father, should we . . . ?" "Father, please . . . ?" Returning from a trip to visit Mollie, I asked the team who went with me to evaluate the experience.

"I like the way they ask about everything," one team member said. "I think we should do more of that asking."

Yes, we should. We should ask about everything. "You do not have," says James 4:2, "because you do not ask."

This business of asking is a mystery, though. Jesus said, "Ask and it will be given to you; seek and you will find; knock and the door will be opened to you. For everyone who asks receives; he who seeks finds; and to him who knocks, the door will be opened" (Matt. 7:7–8). But how do we know what to ask for? What if we are seeking the wrong thing? And some of us have been knocking for so long our knuckles are bloodied. Why doesn't God answer?

I don't know. It's a mystery.

I do know that in the process of asking/ waiting/ listening/ seeking/ knocking, there is something going on in us, and maybe that is the point of the asking in the first place. In asking, we place our friend and our questions in God's hands, which means the matter is out of our hands. Thus it becomes a matter of faith. The longer we leave the matter in God's hands, the longer we watch Him holding it, the more we begin to see the size and power of our Father's hands. The really important question in matters of faith is not what we are asking of God. The question is, do we trust the God whom we are asking?

I have learned about this from a seven-year-old boy named Jacob Lawrence.

Jacob Lawrence and his brother Joshua are members of our church. Their mother Melanie is in my Sunday school class; their dad, Mike, works with my husband Dennis in the Worship Ministry. Jacob Lawrence loves "Mr. Dennis." Every Sunday morning, after the worship service, Jacob and Joshua run up to the edge of the big platform and give Mr. Dennis a great big grin. Several years ago, my husband was in a terrible car crash. Just about everything on him that could be broken or sprained was broken or sprained. Dennis was absent from the worship services for many weeks, and when he was able to come back, in his wheelchair with his many bandages and braces, he was a pretty scary sight. Jacob Lawrence was very concerned.

"We need to pray for Mr. Dennis," Jacob told his mother.

"Yes, we do," said Melanie. "Would you like to pray for him?"

Jacob Lawrence bowed his head, and this is what he prayed: "God, Dennis. Amen."

Oh, the faith of a child. Jacob Lawrence figured God knew what to do with Mr. Dennis.

I have told this story many times in my conferences and felt the refreshing wind of the Spirit as women stood in a circle and one by one prayed, "God, Amy. Amen." "God, Tyler. Amen." "God, my husband. Amen." "God, my boss. Amen." God, my friend. You know what to do with her. Amen.

The journey of faith isn't always a glorious leap; sometimes it's push, pull, or drag. Sometimes we crawl to the steps of the altar and then sit there like a big lump, with nothing to say. Absolutely nothing. In those moments, it is comforting to know that the Spirit of God prays for us. "In the same way, the Spirit helps us in our weakness. We do not know what we ought to pray for, but the Spirit himself intercedes for us with groans that words cannot express. And he who searches our hearts knows the mind of the Spirit, because the Spirit intercedes for the saints in accordance with God's will" (Rom. 8:26–27).

Not only that, but Hebrews 7:24–25 tells us that Jesus *Himself* sits at the right hand of our Father, where He is always interceding for us!

To intercede is to go between two parties. In prayer, I go to God on behalf of my friend. We are pretty good at that part. But the work of intercession is not finished until I also go to my friend on behalf of God. I must speak God's Word to her.

Jesus said, "The words I have spoken to you are spirit and they are life" (John 6:63). In order to grasp the power of Jesus' statement, we must understand a little bit about the importance of the spoken word in ancient times.

According to Hebrew thought patterns, the spoken word had a life of its own. A word, once spoken, had an independent existence. It was not just an idea; it was a happening. When Isaac gave Jacob his blessing, rather than Esau, it was an act, a thing which had been done and could not be taken back. The spoken blessing would have a tangible effect on Jacob's life, and the lack of it on Esau's.

As well, the word, once spoken, had the power to fulfill itself. It could cause itself *to be*. To speak a blessing on someone was to cause them to be blessed. God literally spoke creation into being; He didn't form it out of the mud, like play-dough. "As the rain and the snow come down from heaven, and do not return to it without watering the earth and making it bud and flourish, so that it yields seed for the sower and bread for the eater, so is my word that goes out from my mouth," God says. "It will not return to me empty, but will accomplish what I desire and achieve the purpose for which I sent it" (Isa. 55:10–11).

I have stood before idols in foreign temples, where the presence of evil was palpable. In my hands, I carried index cards that contained Scriptures and prayers given to me by my friends. The words of God, written in the handwriting of my friends at home, was a powerful weapon.

Hattie Cochran had given me Psalm 27:1, "The LORD is my light and my salvation—whom shall I fear? The LORD is the stronghold of my life—of whom shall I be afraid?" Underneath, Hattie had written, "This is true, Karla."

Monica Keathley sent me Revelation 3:8, "See, I have placed before you an open door that no one can shut. I know that you have little strength, yet you have kept my word and have not denied my name."

"You know all the best verses," I e-mailed to her.

"They're all in this book I have!" she replied.

At one particularly difficult moment on that trip, my team and I had arrived exhausted in a foreign city, where we proceeded to navigate our way through the process of taking a taxi to our hotel. The taxi driver shouted at us in a language we couldn't understand as we frantically shoved our bags into the trunk of his car, while his friends stood around us, jeering. Overwhelmed, I stepped back from the fracas and pulled out my stack of index cards. On the top of the pile was this Scripture that Kay Powers had sent to me: "For we are powerless before this great multitude who are coming against us; nor do we know what to do, but our eyes are on You. . . . Thus says the LORD to you, 'Do not fear or be dismayed because of this great multitude, for the battle is not yours but God's. . . . You need not fight in this battle; station yourselves, stand and see the salvation of the LORD on your behalf. . . . Do not fear or be dismayed; tomorrow go out to face them, for the LORD is with you'" (2 Chron. 20:12, 15, 17).

"You alone have the words of life," Peter declared (John 6:68). We must speak them to each other. Because the Word of God is living and active, it demands a response—either obedience in faith or else a plea for more faith. When the angel Gabriel announced God's Word to the virgin Mary that she would be the mother of his Son, Mary replied with both kinds of prayers: "How will this be?" and later, "May it be to me as you have said" (Luke 1:26–38).

God was asking Mary to make a great leap of faith. I find it tender of Him to offer her the gracious, faith-building gift of a friend, Elizabeth: "The angel answered, 'The Holy Spirit will come upon you, and the power of the Most High will overshadow you. So the holy one to be born will be called the Son of God. Even Elizabeth your relative is going to have a child in her old age, and she who was said to be barren is in her sixth month. For nothing is impossible with God'" (Luke 1:35–37).

Luke tells us that as soon as the angel left Mary, she headed straight to Elizabeth's home. "When Elizabeth heard Mary's greeting, the baby leaped in her womb, and Elizabeth was filled with the Holy Spirit. In a loud voice she exclaimed: 'Blessed are you among women, and blessed is the child you will bear! But why am I so favored, that the mother of my Lord should come to me? As soon as the sound of your greeting reached my ears, the baby in my womb leaped for joy. Blessed is she who has believed that what the Lord has said to her will be accomplished!'" (Luke 1:41–45)

Elizabeth's faith was a breath of Spirit-filled air to

Mary. Her words—almost verbatim what the angel Gabriel had said—confirmed the work of God in Mary's life. Elizabeth could respond in this kind of faith because, first, she had experienced the supernatural work of the Spirit in her own miraculous pregnancy; and second, because *she was filled with the Spirit.*

One of the ways in which the Body of Christ navigates the landscape of faith is through the gifts of the Spirit. You cannot live the life of the Spirit without His supernatural power. By definition, a spiritual gift is the supernatural empowering by the Holy Spirit to do a specific work at a specific place and time in a way which only God Himself could do. The gifts of the Spirit are given to all believers for the good of the whole Body (Rom. 12:6–8). God distributes His supernatural ability purposefully. For instance, I do not have much mercy. Have you ever taken those spiritual gift inventories which tell you what your gifts might be? I flunk mercy every time. How embarrassing! I have *no* mercy.

However, if my friend were on her last leg and needed my lap to put her head in, God is completely able to supernaturally gift me with His abundant mercy, which I might pour out on her—and then I might never be merciful again! (And least, not *that* merciful.) My point is, God uses us in supernatural ways to accomplish His supernatural purposes. It's obvious that my friend Debbie Childers has the spiritual gift of teaching—the ability to understand the Bible and make sense of it to others. I call on her when I need help understanding God's Word. My friend Kim has the spiritual gift of giving. Because of her generous gifts of time and resources, I have sometimes been able to join God in what He is doing, when I would not otherwise have been able. Neither of these friends would say, "Oh, yes, I am so good at that." Of course, they know they are not so good at that; God is *so* good in them.

"When the Father chose you all those years ago, it wasn't because you had the equipment to perform the tasks," my friend Lawanna McIver tells me. "He chose you because He knew He could equip you to perform them."

I may not see God's work in me. I may not see that I have such a heart for service or such a capacity to lead others. A deep-spirited friend will call out those gifts. She will say, "That, right there, that's *so* God in you!" She will encourage me to allow the Spirit to develop His supernatural work in me, and to put those spiritual gifts to work in the Body of Christ. A deep-spirited friend will celebrate the presence and power of God in my life.

"Eagerly desire the greater gifts," Paul wrote in 1 Corinthians 12:31. But not all women do.

"I don't want to ask for a spiritual gift," a friend told me. "I might get one I don't want!"

You mean, you might be given something out of your control? Something mysterious? You might be asked to go out on a limb—beyond your ability or understanding?

Yes. A deep-spirited friend will say, "You go, girl." Go with the wind of the Spirit. Deep-spirited friends say "Yes!" to the mysteries of God. And they bless you for believing all things can be accomplished. On the wings of Elizabeth's faith, Mary walked to the edge of the precipice, and Mary not only leapt. She flew.

My deep-spirited friend Esther Burroughs has a way of describing this mysterious movement of the Spirit when it happens in life. She smiles, waves her hand, and makes a sound like this: "Whoosh!" From Esther, I have learned to embrace the "Whoosh!"

Chapter Six
Model Servanthood

And what does the LORD require of you? To act justly and to love mercy and to walk humbly with your God.
—Micah 6:8

On the evening that Jesus conferred upon His disciples the status of friend, He also taught them the lesson of servanthood.

It was just before the Passover Feast. Jesus knew that the time had come for him to leave this world and go to the Father. Having loved his own who were in the world, he now showed them the full extent of his love.

The evening meal was being served, and the devil had already prompted Judas Iscariot, son of Simon, to betray Jesus. Jesus knew that the Father had put all things under his power, and that he had come from God and was returning to God; so he got up from the meal, took off his outer clothing, and wrapped a towel around his waist. After that, he poured water into a basin and began to wash his disciples' feet, drying them with the towel that was wrapped around him.

He came to Simon Peter, who said to him, "Lord, are you going to wash my feet?"

Jesus replied, "You do not realize now what I am doing, but later you will understand."

"No," said Peter, "you shall never wash my feet."

Jesus answered, "Unless I wash you, you have no part with me."

"Then, Lord," Simon Peter replied, "not just my feet but my hands and my head as well!"

Jesus answered, "A person who has had a bath needs only to wash his feet; his whole body is clean. And you are clean, though not every one of you." For he knew who was going to betray him, and that was why he said not every one was clean.

When he had finished washing their feet, he put on his clothes and returned to his place. "Do you understand what I have done for you?" he asked them. "You call me 'Teacher' and 'Lord,' and rightly so, for that is what I am. Now that I, your Lord and Teacher, have washed your feet, you also should wash one another's feet. I have set you an example that you should do as I have done for you. I tell you the truth, no servant is greater than his master, nor is a messenger greater than the one who sent him. Now that you know these things, you will be blessed if you do them. —John 13:1–17

This matter had come up before. It is mentioned in both Luke's Gospel and Mark's (Luke 9:46–48; Mark 9:33–37). John Mark, a close associate of the apostle Peter, is traditionally believed to have recorded Peter's account of Jesus' life and teaching. Luke says that his sources were "many eyewitnesses." Since Luke spent time with Paul in Jerusalem, it's likely that he would have heard both Peter and James talk about their experiences with Christ. All three disciples—Peter, James, and John—had been with Jesus on the mountaintop to witness the Transfiguration, that moment when Jesus appeared in His true heavenly glory, conferring with Moses and Elijah. They had heard the voice of God speak out loud, "This is my Son, whom I have chosen; listen to him." Luke tells us that the three disciples kept this to themselves and told no one else what they had seen (Luke 9:28–36). When the three men came down from the mountain the next day with Jesus, they watched Him cast a demon out of a young boy. Can you blame these three men for being dazzled by such power? And they were in His inner circle! Can't you just picture them, walking along discussing in whispers who among them would be the greatest?

"'There arose a reasoning among them, which should be the greatest' (Luke 9:46). This is enough to destroy a fellowship," wrote Dietrich Bonhoeffer. "Hence it is vitally necessary that every Christian community from the very outset face this dangerous enemy squarely, and eradicate it." That is precisely what Jesus did on the evening of the Passover meal in a dramatic demonstration.

Foot washing was a standard practice of ancient times, just as washing your hands is today. After walking dusty Palestinian roads clad only in sandals, a person's feet would be hot and weary. For both the cleanliness and comfort of his guests, a host provided water by the gate or entrance to his home with which a visitor might wash his own feet. (Most likely the cisterns of water which Jesus turned into wine at the wedding in Cana were intended for this purpose!) Foot washing was considered so lowly a task that it could not be required of a Hebrew slave. So when Jesus removed His own robes, stripping down to the basic garments of a servant, and undertook the act of washing the disciples' feet, they were not only shocked, they recoiled from Him. The very idea of such an action was humiliating to them. But not to Jesus.

Jesus knew who He was and where He was going. John makes that interesting note as He begins the story: "Jesus knew that the Father had put all things under his power, and that he had come from God and was returning to God; so he got up from the meal, took off his outer clothing, and wrapped a towel around his waist" (John 13:3–4).

Because He was secure in His identity, Jesus could step down to place Himself below others and serve them. Jesus' position, His value, His true validation came from God, not men. He did not need to prove Himself; God would do that in time. He *was* God, Paul wrote, but didn't cling to His position. Instead, He made himself nothing. He took on the very form of a servant and humbled Himself. *Therefore* God exalted Him to the highest place (Phil. 2:6–11).

Insecure people do not risk servanthood. They do not lower themselves. Insecure people need to prove themselves. Insecure people are competitive, even with their friends. The apostle Paul understood this. "If anyone has reason to put their confidence in status or credentials, it's me," he told the believers in Philippi. "But whatever was to my profit I now consider it worthless compared to knowing Christ and becoming like Him." Paul went on to say that all who are mature should take such a view of things (Phil. 3:4–15). Where does such maturity come from? From being certain of who you are in Christ.

Paul began his letter to friends in Ephesus by reminding them: this is who you are in Christ. You were chosen by God from the beginning of creation. He knew then that He would give you the status of being called His child. Because of Him you have been redeemed from destruction by Christ's death, forgiven of your sin by His grace. You have been made privy to His plan and purpose in the world. You have been given a role in His plan, called and equipped to join Him in it. You have been marked with the seal of His Holy Spirit. I keep asking that God will open your eyes to see what you have: the hope of being just like Christ, the riches that await you in heaven, the blessings that begin in this life, and the power you have at your disposal to live it! Remember what you used to be, and now see what you are because of what He has done in you and for you. See what you are becoming as God transforms you! *Therefore*, walk worthy. Because this is who you are and what you have in Christ.

Paul instructed his friends not to live as they used to live—not with the same old values, the same old ego and its accompanying needs. Put off that old self, and put on a new self: Christ. Husbands are going to treat wives differently than they used to—and wives, their husbands. Parents and children, servants and masters. "Be imitators of God, therefore, as dearly loved children *[this is who you are]* and live a life of love, just as Christ loved us *[this is how you act]*" (Eph. 5:1–2).

How did Christ love us? He gave Himself up for us. It was a voluntary act. Fellowship between God and man hangs by a slender yet steely thread: God's grace—His choice to have us. God chose to forgive, to love, and to bear with us. "God took men upon Himself and they weighted Him to the ground, but God remained with them and they with God," wrote Bonhoeffer. "In bearing with men God maintained fellowship with them."

The old-fashioned word for God's action is *condescend*. It is a word which has taken on a negative meaning in our culture because it has been exhibited in the wrong spirit. To condescend is to lower yourself from your particular (or rightful) status in order to deal with someone who is inferior. This sounds distasteful to most people, and we do it with distaste. We make it clear that we are being inconvenienced. But God does not. God graciously lowered Himself to man's level in Jesus Christ.

What would motivate God to do that? Love. Servanthood—Godly condescension—flows out of a genuine interest in and love for the other person. The fact that a friendship is a chosen relationship makes it fragile. Love—Christlike love—is the only thing which gives our friendship the elasticity and strength to survive the inevitable tests that come our way. That Christlike, condescending love is what we term *servanthood*.

Servanthood enables us to bear with a friend even when we are angered by or disappointed in her. "Disappointment is inevitable for one reason," says Ann Hibbard. "We can only have sinners for friends." A friend is going to hurt you. She is going to let you down. She is going to mess up, and you are going to be sometimes mildly irritated and sometimes horribly, horribly wounded. The question is not, *Will* she? The question is, What will you do about it *when* she does?

"Therefore, as God's chosen people, holy and dearly loved, clothe yourselves with compassion, kindness, humility, gentleness and patience. Bear with each other and forgive whatever grievances you may have against one another. Forgive as the Lord forgave you. And over all these virtues put on love, which binds them all together in perfect unity. Let the peace of Christ rule in your hearts, since as members of one body you were called to peace" (Col. 3:12–15).

In their book *I Know Just What You Mean*, Ellen Goodman and Patricia O'Brien talk frankly about a painful moment in their lifelong friendship, when Ellen's thoughtless act wounded Pat. Pat's first impulse was to react in anger. "It was a very tempting option," she says. "But underneath the desire to react this way was something steadier. Did I act only on what had just happened, or on the deep reality of the whole friendship? Did I really believe I was suddenly rejected, or was I experiencing the nasty surprise of realizing even your best friend can do something dumb?"

It is a nasty surprise when your friend does something dumb—or even deliberate. For believers who are friends, that "something steadier" which keeps us from reacting solely based on our feelings is the steady love of God, "who reconciled us to himself through Christ and gave us the ministry of reconciliation" (2 Cor. 5:18).

Andy Stanley, pastor of North Point Community Church in Atlanta, Georgia, asks this question: "Do I want to be right, or do I want a relationship? Which is more important to me?" Andy discusses this in a sermon entitled "Rx for the Fractured Family, Part Four: Take Only as Directed":

> We pursue reconciliation because God did that for us. So let's clarify the goal: The point is not for the other to see your side and agree with you that you are right. The point of reconciliation is that we accept each other in spite of our differences. I don't have to stand outside the door of reconciliation until you get your act together. There are no conditions for reconciliation, because God put no conditions on our reconciliation. While we were still sinners, Christ died for us (Rom. 5:8).
>
> But then, aren't I condoning your sin? Well, Jesus invited Matthew to eat with Him; He ate with sinners. Our concern for the individual must outweigh the offense we take to their sin. Why? Because

reconciliation leads to relationship, and relationship leads to influence. What if God had stood back because we were unholy? There would be no salvation. He would remain holy, and we would not have opportunity to know Him and thus be made holy. If I just want to be right, I can stand outside and make a point. But people are not changed by us standing outside and making a point. They are changed by relationship and influence.

The real obstacle to reconciliation is not what my sister did, but my unwillingness to choose or endure a difficult or painful relationship. "Ask yourself," Stanley says, "what is it that's keeping you from accepting the other person?"

It might be that my friend has not asked for forgiveness. It is easy to forgive a friend who comes to me in humility, asking for my forgiveness. But what if she's not sorry? Am I still expected to forgive her? Yes.

When Peter asked Jesus, "Lord, how many times shall I forgive my brother when he sins against me? Up to seven times?" Jesus answered, "I tell you, not seven times, but seventy-seven times" (Matt. 18:21–22). In rabbinic discussion, the consensus was that a person might be forgiven a repeated sin three times; on the fourth, there was no forgiveness. Peter, thinking himself big-hearted, volunteered "seven times" in answer to his own question. It was a good start, but Jesus wanted him to think bigger.

Jesus' response alluded to Genesis 4:24, an ancient poem of revenge called the Song of Lamech. Lamech was a descendent of Cain. Cain harbored so much resentment against his brother Abel that he killed him. Five generations later, revenge was still a way of life for Cain's descendants. "If Cain got his revenge seven times," declared Lamech, "I'm going to get mine seventy times seven." Jesus used this ancient illustration to introduce a new principle of forgiveness.

*T*o forgive requires that my heart want two things: to be right with God and to be free of resentment. I must want that more than I want to hang on to my hurt feelings, even if I have a right to them. Servanthood—condescending love—lays down its rights. Like the right to revenge. God is righteous; that's a part of His character. His righteousness means that He will be faithful to keep His word. He will be faithful to defend the right. Do I trust God's character? Then I will place my hurts in His hands and allow Him to deal with the unfairness of my situation.

Here's another thing: It may be years before my friend ever sees that she was wrong. Am I willing to cripple my relationship with God for that long? Because that's what I'm doing. "When you stand praying, if you hold anything against anyone, forgive him, so that your Father in heaven may forgive you your sins" (Mark 11:25). As long as I hold on to my resentment, I wall off a part of my heart from God. I refuse to obey His command to forgive. Now I've got much bigger problems to deal with than the wrong my friend may have done to me! Do you see that God requires forgiveness of us, not just for the sake of our friendship, but for the health of our own souls?

"When you reconcile with a person, you reconcile with all their baggage, consequences, and problems—their junk," says Andy Stanley. "This is the 'cringe point'—when God wants to do something *in you*, not just *for* the other person. The cringe point is where you decide if you want to shed your nature and take on Christ's nature, who shouldered our sins at the cross. Quite often, moving me past my cringe factor, thus building in me more of Christ's nature, is God's purpose in reconciliation. Allow God to finish what He started in you, and then it will be clear what you should do regarding the other person."

Servanthood—condescending love—enables me to bear with my friend in moments of crisis and avoid the urge to fix her. In fact, precisely because it is natural, it is probably not right. Our natural impulse does not arise from Christ's nature, but from our human nature. If your first impulse is to fix your friend, resist it.

Ann Hibbard recalls with gratitude the way her friend Martha dealt with her in a time of crisis: "Last fall when I was going through a particularly dark and painful time with one of my children, I met Martha for breakfast and shared with her the details. I knew that I didn't need to hold back anything from her. Her love for me and my family and her intimate knowledge of us qualified her as a trustworthy friend. I felt completely safe to disclose these things to her, because I knew that she would not respond in a way that would make it difficult for me. . . . Martha did not cajole or advise me. She listened with great empathy, feeling my pain along with me. After listening for the better part of an hour, she asked me if I wanted any input."

Ann could be so open with Martha because she knew that Martha would not be hard on her. Her friendship with Martha was a safe space. "A turtle sticks his head back into his shell when he is threatened," says Andy Stanley. "Likewise, when the other person does not feel safe, they won't come out. They may not trust that you will not wound them."

My friend Ruth had this experience with her brand new sister-in-law. When Jenny married Ruth's brother, Ruth hoped they would become close friends. But when Ruth's brother and his new wife went through a crisis in their marriage, Ruth said some things to Jenny she shouldn't have said.

"My attitudes and speech were haughty, selfish, and ugly when they should not have been," Ruth admits. "Unfortunately, my heart was not prepared to respond in a godly fashion. I tried to tell her what *I* thought she should do."

Jenny was hurt, and she shut Ruth out. She wouldn't take Ruth's calls, and she did not respond to the note Ruth sent asking for her forgiveness. Brokenhearted, Ruth turned to her brother for advice.

"He said, 'Well, I wouldn't send Jenny any more notes with Bible verses on them.' He told me that Jenny considers me a big hypocrite because I send her note cards with Bible verses on them, but I acted so harshly to her. Jenny feels like I'm saying, 'I'm good; I read my Bible, but you're not.' Boy, has she misread my heart!"

Unfortunately, those of us with well-intentioned hearts often rush in to help our friend through a crisis, when what she needs is someone to be with her—just be *with* her—in the midst of it. Fixing is, in essence, interrupting. It's saying, "Let's get on with this." Love—condescending love, servant love—is not in a hurry. Love "bears all things, believes all things, hopes all things, endures all things" (1 Cor. 13:7). Fixing others is not a biblical imperative; loving them is.

"But I want to be useful," you might say. I do, too. I think this makes me a valuable friend. But usefulness is not the point in friendship. When my usefulness becomes paramount, I am no longer functioning as a servant; I am hankering to be master. Usefulness is an issue of control, not value.

"The serious Christian . . . is likely to bring with him a very definite idea of what Christian life together should be and to try to realize it," wrote Dietrich Bonhoeffer.

"But God's grace speedily shatters such dreams." Bonhoeffer called these presuppositions "wish dreams":

> *Every human wish dream that is injected into the Christian community is a hindrance to genuine community and must be banished if genuine community is to survive. He who loves his dream of a community more than the Christian community itself becomes a destroyer of the latter, even though his personal intentions may be ever so honest and earnest and sacrificial.*
>
> *God hates visionary dreaming; it makes the dreamer proud and pretentious. The man who fashions a visionary ideal of community demands that it be realized by God, by others, and by himself. When things do not go his way, he calls the effort a failure. When his ideal picture is destroyed, he sees the community going to smash. So he becomes, first an accuser of his brethren, then an accuser of God, and finally the despairing accuser of himself.*
>
> *Because God has already laid the only foundation of our fellowship, because God has bound us together in one body with other Christians in Jesus Christ, long before we entered into common life with them, we enter into that common life not as demanders but as thankful recipients.*

*T*o be a thankful recipient of Christian friendship is to lovingly receive all that my friend's life brings my way—her frailties and oddities which try my patience, her way of doing things, which may not match mine. I embrace her individuality, the gifts and talents with which she is endowed, the stage of life in which she finds herself, the people to whom she is bound. Servanthood requires of me that I honor these other commitments in her life. I cannot demand that she be my friend exclusively, or that our friendship be given first place. Rightfully, a husband, a child, a parent comes first. At times, they may leave little of her for me. That you give a friendship priority during one period of your life and not another is not at all unusual. Life changes; the needs and demands of a friendship change. A true friend rolls with it.

I have three sons, which means I am constantly adjusting my attention to who needs what. This past year, a great deal of the attention has been given to our oldest son Seth. In April, we celebrated his eighteenth birthday, closely followed by a round of parties and activities leading up to high school graduation in May. The month of June was consumed with sorting, packing, and moving Seth to college in time for the second term of summer school. On July 1, we loaded our van and his Jeep, and all of us made the long trip to Texas. We spent the next day unpacking and running back and forth to Target for things we'd forgotten.

"I'm tired," my youngest son Ben complained about three o'clock that afternoon.

"So am I," I said, "but today is Seth's day. We're going to think about Seth today."

"It's been Seth's day for three months!" Ben said, exasperated. "When is it going to be my day?"

Because friendship involves two lives, and the many worlds within those lives, there will be times when it is your day and times when it is my day. Servanthood—condescending love—enables me to celebrate your life as fully as if it were mine. Sometimes that means shouldering your burdens. Sometimes that means applauding your joy.

When Seth graduated from high school, there were several women who claimed a share of the happiness. Saralu was there when he was born and has celebrated every one of his birthdays. This past year, she literally prayed him into Baylor University. Amie was Seth's babysitter during the last years of her single life and her first years of marriage. She practiced on him until her own children came along. Vicki has spent almost every major holiday and vacation with us. Karen became his unofficial aunt. Our joke is, Karen always has gum! His official aunt, Kim, has been his second mother, ferrying him to and from school and doctor's appointments, tutoring him in math, advising us through the process of applying for college.

All of these women came to love Seth because they

loved me, and Seth is a part of who I am. They love Matt and Ben and Dennis, too. They put up with more than their share of inconvenience because my family demands a great deal of me. In fact, they enable me to meet those demands, and sometimes I know they lay aside their own commitments to help me fulfill mine. This is what servant friends do. We pray for each other, cook for each other, rescue each other, cheer for each other. Henry David Thoreau wrote about these kinds of friends, "They cherish each other's hopes. They are kind to each other's dreams."

Some of my friends live far away, but we are still able to cherish each other's hopes and dreams through phone calls and e-mails, clippings and photos sent in the mail. I paste my friends' e-mailed prayer requests into my journal. My journal is a patchwork quilt, much like my life. It's not organized into sections or divided by topics. Some people have a prayer journal, and a separate daily diary, and a journal for quotes and Bible verses. Not me. I have what looks like a third grader's science project. It has notes from my children pasted in it and e-mails stuffed between the pages of handwritten notes. Bible verses are scribbled in margins, prayers jotted in the corners. My friends' requests are just jammed in there with the rest of my life.

One reason I like this method (if it can be called a method) is that it takes my focus off me, me, me. It moves others' lives in front of mine. Their concerns become my concerns as their lives get intertwined with mine. I come to a blank page of this journal because I am tired or confused or just plain whiny. I think I will sort things out, think them through, by writing my thoughts and feelings down. But it gets old quickly, this bellyaching navel-gazing. Turn the pages: same old struggles. Same old sins. Same old lists. Blah, blah, blah. Ah! Here is someone else's questions, someone else's pain. To be quite honest, sometimes I do think, "Thank God I don't have to deal with *that*."

On really good days, my heart opens to them for all the right reasons. I am generous enough to lift their burdens or joys and hold them up to the Father. It's a privilege, but it's also a blessing—at times, a relief—to go to God with a different challenge, another's concern. Often, quite often, I find that God meets my own measly needs as I flex new muscles of faith on behalf of my friend. And maybe, just maybe, that was His intent all along.

Chapter Seven

Keep Me Involved

Yes, LORD, walking in the way of your laws, we wait for you; your name and renown are the desire of our hearts.
—Isaiah 26:8

She changed my life from the moment she stepped into it. She literally rocked my world with the first words out of her mouth. I was utterly captivated. I was hooked. Ba-da-bing! I loved this woman and wanted to know her. So I, well . . . stalked her until we became friends, mostly by e-mail. Then the twins came along, with the whole ordeal of the adoption process, as agonizing as labor. And the late night prayers flew back and forth, halfway around the world.

There was never any small talk, even in the beginning of our friendship. I dove into the deep waters with her. If she has frustration these days, it is because she feels she is wading in the shallow waters of raising kids, keeping house, getting through runny noses and all-nighters, while her husband continues the deep work of missions. I tell her that her tasks are not in the shallow end of the pool. She is definitely in the deep end, and just as over her head with three toddlers as she is with a whole country of people who don't know Christ.

One night, I heard the voice of this dear friend on the phone from half a world away. One year ago, Sheryl had said, "Come over here." True to form, she cut to the chase: "It's nice that you pray for our work, but that's nothing like walking among the people." So on this night, I huddled around the speakerphone with the five women who were going with me on the trip. They were hearing Sheryl's voice for the first time. These women, also my friends, had prayed for Sheryl, rearranged their lives, and stepped out in faith to join her in her work. That night, she became more than "Karla's friend" to them; she became flesh and blood. What a *wow* moment!

Our lives connect other lives, like links in a chain. When I was a girl, I would lie in the grass and make clover chains, weaving together their long stems. That is what God does with us, weaving a circle of friendships, connections, and shared passions and experiences. That night I was the link between these women. After this trip, they would be bound to each other and to a common passion: love for these people who do not know Christ.

The Greek philosopher Aristotle believed that a true friendship involved a commitment to the common good. That is never more true than when applied to a Christian friendship, for the follower of Christ is engaged not only in the pursuit of her own spiritual growth but is committed to a community of believers and, beyond that, engaged in God's work of reconciling the world to Himself. We cannot forget that. We cannot reduce our friendship to a circle of "Jesus and me" or "Jesus and me and you." We must remember that we are engaged in something larger than that, with Someone larger than we are, the One who created the universe, who passionately loves everyone and everything in it.

> Just then his disciples returned and were surprised to find him talking with a woman. But no one asked, "What do you want?" or "Why are you talking with her?"
>
> Then, leaving her water jar, the woman went back to the town and said to the people, "Come, see a man who told me everything I ever did. Could this be the Christ?" They came out of the town and made their way toward him.
>
> Meanwhile his disciples urged him, "Rabbi, eat something."

But he said to them, "I have food to eat that you know nothing about."

Then his disciples said to each other, "Could someone have brought him food?"

"My food," said Jesus, "is to do the will of him who sent me and to finish his work. Do you not say, 'Four months more and then the harvest'? I tell you, open your eyes and look at the fields! They are ripe for harvest." —John 4:27–35

Just picture it: As the little Samaritan woman ran from the well back to her village, the disciples returned bearing lunch. I find it quite honest of John to admit that none of them were all that curious about why Jesus had been talking to her. They were hungry. Jesus, always with His eye on the larger picture, was concerned with another kind of hunger: spiritual hunger. He had seen it in this woman's eyes.

"Look out there," he said to his disciples, pointing to the fields of shoulder-high wheat. "The fields are white with harvest." Between the stalks of waving grain came the white-cloaked heads of the men in the village, led by the Samaritan woman who brought them out to see the man she thought might be the Messiah. "Many of the Samaritans from that town believed in him because of the woman's testimony, 'He told me everything I ever did.' So when the Samaritans came to him, they urged him to stay with them, and he stayed two days. And because of his words many more became believers" (John 4:39–41).

There was indeed a harvest, and there is today. Jesus constantly has to raise the eyes of His disciples to look up and see the larger world. We begin by seeing the greatness of the God who is at work in it.

"I wish I could tell my best friend how important coming to church can be for Christians, for our growth," one woman wrote to me. "I cannot tell her this because she seems to have a million excuses." Yes, we can have a million excuses for not coming to church to worship. Too busy. Too tired. Too many weekend commitments. After a week in the workplace, we're just not up for another meeting. But when the Body of Christ comes together, it is not just another meeting; it is a meeting with God.

"It is by the grace of God that a congregation is permitted to gather visibly in this world to share God's Word and sacrament," wrote Dietrich Bonhoeffer while living in an underground German Christian community during the reign of Adolf Hitler. "Not all Christians receive this blessing. The imprisoned, the sick, the scattered lonely, the proclaimers of the Gospel in heathen lands stand alone. They know that visible fellowship is a blessing. They remember, as the Psalmist did, how they went 'with the multitude . . . to the house of God, with the voice of joy and praise, with a multitude that kept holy day' (Psalm 42:4)."

The early church was marked by its sense of joy and exhilaration because of God's presence and power. "Everyone was filled with awe," Luke described in Acts 2:43. Two chapters later, Luke recorded what happened when Peter and John healed a man crippled from birth and then proceeded to preach the gospel to those who had witnessed the miracle in the temple courts. Peter and John were imprisoned for their action, then warned not to speak of Jesus Christ again. Their reply? "We cannot stop speaking about what we have seen and heard!"

"After further threats they let them go," Luke wrote. "They could not decide how to punish them, because all the people were praising God for what had happened" (Acts 4:21).

"On their release, Peter and John went back to their own people and reported all that the chief priests and elders had said to them. When they heard this, they raised their voices together in prayer to God. 'Sovereign Lord,' they said, 'you made the heaven and the earth and the sea, and everything in them'" (Acts 4:23–24).

The first act of this group of friends was not to run for cover, not to fret for Peter and John's safety—not even to ask God for ease or protection. Their first act was to worship: to remember Who was really in charge. The first words out of their mouths declared this: "Sovereign Lord." In Greek, *despotes*—the master of the house. In worship, we acknowledge who is the Master of the house. We affirm that God has absolute authority. "For life's basic decision is rarely, if ever, whether to believe in God or not, but whether to worship or compete with him," writes Eugene Peterson.

*I*t is a sure sign that my friend has begun to compete with God when she neglects the discipline of worship. For it *is* a discipline, a continual coming back to bow the knee and confess, "You are in charge, God." When we forget that and begin to think it is all up to us, we become first discouraged, then isolated, then defeated. Alone, we are easy prey for Satan, who as George Swimmock says, "watches for those vessels that sail without a convoy." Discouragement is just the first step in the process of my friend's faith being dismantled.

Think of what happened at the World Trade Center on September 11, 2001. A plane struck an upper floor of a tower, demolishing that section of the building, but the tower remained. Then fire began to spread (the fire a byproduct of the collision), eating away at the infrastructure, until floor by floor, like an accordion, the building collapsed.

So the process of losing faith happens. I am hit by a blow. At first, the wound may be considerable, but it is contained. Then slowly, anger and doubt begin to burn. A great "Why?" resonates throughout me and begins to bang on the walls of other rooms in my heart. A smoldering fire begins. It spreads. Some people are destroyed in this way; they literally implode, collapsing in on themselves. In others, a cold fear sets in—a killing frost that hardens chamber after chamber of the heart. We close each door to warmth. And die.

"We must pay more careful attention, therefore, to what we have heard, so that we do not drift away," said the writer of Hebrews. "See to it, brothers, that none of you has a sinful, unbelieving heart that turns away from the living God. But encourage one another daily, as long as it is called Today, so that none of you may be hardened by sin's deceitfulness" (Heb. 2:1, 3:12–13). As your friend, I have to be proactive at the first sign of discouragement. If I wait until the process of demolition has its way, you may have already become too hardened to hear the truth.

This has happened often to me with friends who were going through a divorce. They have hidden the first stages of their struggle so well that I did not know about their battle until they announced their intention. By then, the process had gone too far. No one was listening. The building had already disintegrated; what remained was just the collapse.

"Let us not give up meeting together, as some are in the habit of doing," says Hebrews 10:25, "but let us encourage one another—and all the more as you see the Day approaching."

As the day to depart on our trip to work with Sheryl approached, each of the women on our team was wracked by our own discouragement. Kellie's childcare became an issue. Betty's already frail father began to appear more frail. Kim received an abnormal mammogram. I felt the fear closing in all around. At such times, it becomes necessary for us to encourage each other all the more, rather than draw away from each other, as we are inclined to do.

We do this by deploying the weapon of worship. This is what the believers in Jerusalem did when Peter and John were returned to them. First, they acknowledged the Sovereign Lord was in control. Then they recalled the great things He had done in the past. "'Sovereign Lord,' they said, 'you made the heaven and the earth and the sea, and everything in them. You spoke by the Holy Spirit through the mouth of your servant, our father David: "Why do the nations rage and the peoples plot in vain? The kings of the earth take their stand and the rulers gather together against the Lord and against his Anointed One." Indeed Herod and Pontius Pilate met together with the Gentiles and the people of Israel in this city to conspire against your holy servant Jesus, whom you anointed. They did what your power and will had decided beforehand should happen'" (Acts 4:24–28).

"From memory comes hope," my pastor Mike Glenn says. "From hope comes a behavior that anticipates a future reality." In one of his sermons, Mike pointed to the story of Joshua and his army marching around the walls of Jericho (Josh. 6:1–20): "God said to walk around the walls for six days. The first few days, their focus was on the size of the walls. On the fourth day or so, one of them began to remember history—how God had delivered other kingdoms, other armies, other cities into their hands. As the people walked and remembered, they began to focus on God's greatness, not the size of Jericho's walls. So by the seventh day, they were ready to shout! The weapon God gave Joshua was worship. Jericho's walls crumbled under the weight of God's glory."

When we worship together, God's glory is not only displayed *to* us, but in and through us. When Peter and John were hauled before the leaders of the temple to explain the miracle they had performed, the temple authorities "saw the courage of Peter and John and realized that they were unschooled, ordinary men," says Acts 4:13. "They were astonished and they took note that these men had been with Jesus."

It is noticeable when we have been with Jesus. As the apostle Paul described it, through us God "spreads everywhere the fragrance of the knowledge of him. For we are to God the aroma of Christ among those who are being saved and those who are perishing. To the one we are the smell of death; to the other, the fragrance of life" (2 Cor. 2:14–16).

The practice of worship in any religion has certain sounds and smells, an ambiance. When Sheryl prepared my team to visit her people, she said, "The first thing you will notice is the smell. It's what you will take away with you when you go home. It will cling to your clothes and

your suitcases and every object you bring back with you."
She was right. On my desk, I have a wooden box I purchased at a stall outside a large temple when I was there.
When I open it, I can smell the place.

In biblical times, those who worshiped in Jerusalem went up the great hill to the Temple. Inside its walls, there were stalls of sheep, goats, lambs, doves. There were altars of fire, and the smell of the flesh and blood of the animals offered there. A worshiper left the temple with the smell of worship clinging to his robes—charred flesh, smoke and incense, the smell of an ancient city. David longed for these smells when he, hiding out from Saul's army, could not go to worship. Isaiah saw God face-to-face here and walked away with the smell of his own charred lips, purified by the angel's burning coal. Jesus walked up this hill and into its gates, smelling the scent of His own future, the Lamb of God, the final sacrifice.

When we worship, we go out with the smell of death clinging to us—the death of pride, of self-sufficiency, the death of sin. That is the charred scent of those parts of us being burned away in order to make room for the life of Christ. To those who do not confess, "Jesus is Lord," this is an unwelcome smell. It is a distasteful odor, the scent of pain and fear. To those who confess Him, who worship Him, it is the familiar smell of His presence. In either case, there is no fragrance clinging to us unless we have been in worship. There is no knowledge of Him unless we have been with Him.

Those who love us encourage us to take the time to be in the presence of Christ. They hold us in the pain of being seared. They comfort us in the burning away of self. And they welcome the accompanying smells.

When Peter and John returned from their experience in the temple, their friends did not run right back to confront those who had opposed them. First they knelt. First they worshiped. First they prayed. Peter and John came back to their friends exhilarated but exhausted. Wisely, their friends knew they needed to be taken into the presence of the Sovereign Lord.

Too many of us encourage our sister in Christ to run out there and conquer the world. We admire her when she does acts of service, when she is a bold witness. We put her on a pedestal when she wears herself out serving faithfully. We do not often take into account how much it costs her to bear witness to Christ. We rarely say, "Go into the inner court." We rarely say, "Go one-on-one with Him." And even fewer of us walk into that court full of smoke and flame alongside her. But when we do, we arm her with the mighty weapon of worship.

We do this by encouraging each other to get away with God—to take a walk, an afternoon, a weekend. We say, "I will watch your kids while you go," or we say, "Go with me" to this worship service or concert or retreat. I meet women all over the country when I am teaching at retreats, friends who come together year after year to get away. They get up early for sunrises. They attend seminars. They laugh over lunch, sneak away for naps, linger over dinner. They sing with all their hearts in worship, and they stay up late giggling into the wee hours of the night. One of the great joys of my work is to see these groups of friends arrive a little exhausted, but full of anticipation, then leave relaxed and refreshed. There is just nothing like being in the presence of God and women!

It doesn't have to be that organized. One of my favorite worship experiences was a makeshift communion supper of leftover foccacia bread and cranberry juice with my beach friends. We carted it out to the beach on our bikes, spread out our blanket, and said the tender and binding words, "This is My body broken for you." Then we fed the remains of our sacraments to the seagulls! It was a moment of joy for us.

The point is to engage my friend with God, to get the two of them face-to-face. I may do it with the simple gift of a diary or devotional. I have a friend who gives the most wonderful gift: a quiet time basket. She fills it with all the essentials for a daily time of prayer and worship—a daily devotional book or prayer guide, a blank journal, a nice pen. Some note cards and stamps. A tape or CD of worshipful music. And of course, tissues! It's her gentle way of lifting her friends' eyes to see the horizon, where God awaits.

The point is to get my friend and God talking to each other, because talking to God will change my friend's life. At first she'll be shy. Then she'll talk about herself, her children, her husband, her work. Gradually, if my friend spends enough time with God, her world will widen. God will talk to her about His family, His children, *His* work. Pretty soon she'll be praying for people halfway around the world.

I'm always amazed, after I've spoken about my friends around the world, when women say, "I would love to pray for missionaries, but I don't know how." *Well how do you pray for yourself?* That's what I reply. *What are your daily concerns, your petty concerns, your nighttime fears, your daytime worries?* Pray for them the same way. They are just women. I say this with patience, because at one time, I didn't know how to pray for the world, either. My problem was not small prayers, but a small life. I just didn't have a window on the world. How did I get it? I became friends with some women whose windows were wider, who invited me into their lives, and I came to enjoy the view.

"We were at dinner last evening with some friends," says Eugene Peterson. "Conversation more or less circled around fixing the world, and their disappointing experiences in making a difference. . . . And here's the thing that struck me in the middle of the conversation; not a word in the conversation indicated any awareness of what Christ is doing or has done." Peterson described this conversation with some surprise, but it happens all the time. What do we talk about around the dinner table, over coffee, as we're jogging or driving or shopping or waiting in line? We discuss the events of our day, what this or that person said or did, what we are planning to do about our job/ house/ children/ weekend/ future. Do we add, "And this is what I saw God doing"? Do we ask each other how Christ's agenda fits into our plans? Do we exclaim over the one million miraculous things He has done all around us in the course of the day? Because that is what He has been doing.

My friend Maribeth and her husband Jeremy called this week to ask, "Can we tell you a story?" Maribeth and Jeremy belong to our church. They sing in our choir; they are talented musicians, gifted worship leaders, and this is what they long to do as their work. Just two weeks ago, over lunch with my husband, Jeremy was asking, "Why hasn't it happened for us? Why am I still in this computer job that I hate?" Dennis very wisely said, "I don't know the answer to that question, Jeremy. But I do know that God works in His way at His time for a reason. We'll just have to try and understand the reason."

A week later, our community was stunned by the death of a young and brilliant Christian musician, Grant Cunningham. Grant was killed in a senseless accident; he was playing soccer with a bunch of guys when he collided with the goalie and was knocked unconscious. Grant went into a coma and never regained consciousness. He died a few days later, leaving behind a wife and three small sons. All of us in the Christian music community were shocked. And we asked ourselves over and over, "What was the point?"

On the Monday morning after Grant died, Jeremy was at his desk, at the job he so disliked. His boss said, "Listen, if Brian is acting strangely today, cut him some slack, okay? He was involved in a game last weekend where a guy died."

Jeremy just knew there couldn't have been that many sports accidents over the holiday weekend. So when he had the opportunity, he stopped by his coworker Brian's desk and said gently, "Listen, I heard about what happened. Was that the accident with Grant Cunningham? I'm so sorry. That must have been really scary. If you need anybody to talk to, I'm here."

Brian looked up at him with tears in his eyes.

"You don't understand, Jeremy," he replied. "I'm the goalie. I'm the one who hit him."

Jeremy's heart broke for Brian. He didn't know whether Brian believed in God or not, but Jeremy told Brian he believed that God was doing something powerful in Brian's life.

"I will be praying that God will reveal the larger purpose for your life," Jeremy said.

Grant Cunningham's funeral was held on Wednesday morning. The church was packed; there was literally standing room only. Most of the people there were involved in some way with Grant in the Christian music industry. But as Jeremy and Maribeth looked around the room, they spotted one guy who didn't quite fit in. He obviously wasn't a "musician type." He was standing way in the back, all by himself. Jeremy realized it was Brian, and he went to stand by Brian's side.

That afternoon, Brian came to Jeremy's desk at work. He told Jeremy that he'd been reading a lot of things about God lately. And then at Grant's funeral, he had heard a lot more. He didn't really understand it all; he had a lot of questions, but he felt that God was trying to say something to him.

Jeremy looked at Brian a long time.

"Brian," he asked, "do you believe that God could love you so much that He would go to these lengths to let you know it?"

That night at our choir rehearsal, Jeremy stood weeping before his family of friends and believers. "I know now why I'm still in this job," he said. And together, we bowed our heads as Jeremy prayed for Brian to come to know and believe in the love of God.

I have seen a community of friends—believers—who see God's work *that* specifically in their daily lives *all the time*. These friends live quietly and joyfully in a country where Christianity is a covert lifestyle. They do not set up great ministries or build church buildings. They do not do Christian things with Christian names on them. My friends go about their daily lives, they plant seeds, and they watch. They observe God.

I sat with them at dinner one night in their private quarters. This was family night for them, the night of the week when they all get to be together. They cook their favorite foods for this meal; on this night, it was Tex Mex. I watched their faces around the table, relaxed, laughing, teasing each other lovingly, sharing the good joke. Family night is also the night they talk about their week—where they have been, who they have seen, what they talked about. I listened as the conversation became quieter, more thoughtful. One member relayed her conversation with a fellow student who is asking a lot of questions about the meaning of life.

"She asked me how I make decisions about my future," the girl at our table said.

"Hmm," said another. "Do you think the Father is opening a door?"

"I hope so!" she replied. "I asked for an opportunity to talk about Him."

Right there, right at the table, reaching across the tortillas and refried beans, they all joined hands and asked God to make this the opportunity for a conversation about Him. Then they went on around the table, turning over the week's events, looking for the ways in which God is working, asking Him to open doors. I was reminded of that group of friends in Acts 4, to which Peter and John returned after their adventures at the Temple. I imagine that group, gathered over flat bread and figs, hanging on Peter and John's every word, listening to them recount their conversations, marveling at the miracles God had performed, applauding their friends' courage. I see them reach across the bowls of olives and cups of wine to join hands. And I remember the results: "After they prayed, the place where they were meeting was shaken. And they were all filled with the Holy Spirit and spoke the word of God boldly" (Acts 4:31).

We can do this, you and I. We can train ourselves to look for God's action in the world. We can dare to ask Him to open doors, to give us opportunities to speak His Word boldly. We can ask Him for miracles. We can watch for them, and we can thank Him when we see them come to pass. We can bow the knee and say to Him, "Sovereign Lord." We can look out beyond our small lives to see the bigger picture. We can ask each other, "Do you see Him working?" We can unleash His power upon the whole wide world.

We can do it. Listen, all it takes is two friends who reach across the table and join hands.

Chapter Eight
On the Journey

Do two walk together unless
they have agreed to do so?
—Amos 3:3

I thank God for "the amazing Jesus-gift of 'friend,'" as Eugene Peterson calls it. For Christians are not "of this world." We are aliens here, those of us who belong to the kingdom of God, and we often feel it. How would we ever make it without others who, like us, have the mind and Spirit of Christ?

"We necessarily live so much of our lives in exile, so to be able to spot the people and places that reestablish our true identity is so important," wrote Peterson in *The*

Wisdom of Each Other. "Aren't we lucky to have so many visible confirmations of the invisible graces within us?"

You may have read this book and thought of the names and faces of those friends who are "Jesus-gifts" to you. *Yes, you have said to me, I know just what you mean.* Perhaps some of you are not feeling so lucky. You are wondering, *Where do I get such a friend? How will I find someone who will walk the journey of faith with me?*

First, you must walk the journey yourself. First and foremost, you must be a person who belongs to God, who has determined to live the confession, "Jesus is Lord." No friend, however she may be given to you by God, is responsible for your own spiritual disciplines of Bible study, prayer, confession, obedience, worship, and service. You are.

Second, you must be this kind of friend. Don't wait for someone to come along and say, "Hey, how about we start holding each other accountable for holy lives?" Go ahead and live one. "Be completely humble and gentle," Paul wrote to his friends in Ephesus. "Make it your priority to preserve unity. Use your gifts. Put off your old nature and take on Christ's. Tell the truth, and do it lovingly. Control your anger. Don't steal. Don't gossip or slander. Don't hold onto bitterness and envy. Be kind and compassionate." Paul summed it up into one sentence when he said, "Imitate Christ" (Eph. 4:20–5:1, my paraphrase). Go ahead and put this lifestyle into practice in the friendships you already have. As long as you are willing to dish the dirt, your friends will be, too. So lift the bar. Set a new standard.

Third, ask God for godly friends. Pray for the friends you already have. Pray for their spiritual growth. Ask God to give them a burden for the same kind of relationship that you want. And ask God to send women into your life who can be this kind of friend. Ask Him to place in your life women who want to grow up together in Christ.

The friends I have came to me in different ways. Saralu Lunn and I became friends because our husbands were friends. We had not one thing in common except for *that* when we first met twenty-two years ago. Kim Cox and I became friends because she married my brother. Vicki Dvoracek and I bonded over our mutual love for music and drama in our church. Susan Wommack's husband and I were friends in college; when I met Susan years later, we were instant buddies. Amy Morse and I are neighbors; our children practically live in each other's homes. Debbie Childers and I met at a women's retreat in Alabama. Esther Burroughs has been my mentor in professional Christian ministry as well as my friend. Laura Savage and Monica Keathley became my dear friends over the years we have worked together in women's missions. Barbara Curnutt and I share a passion for the same people group in a vastly unsaved area of the world. My friend Sheryl and I cemented our friendship by e-mail. She introduced me to Mollie, who became a fast friend, too. Together, they introduced me to a part of the world I now love and pray for daily.

Some of these friends I see every day. They know where the dishes are in my kitchen cabinets. They are what you call "back door" friends. Some friends I see only once or twice a year. We stay in touch by e-mail and phone. Our lives are woven together because we have agreed to do so. We have forged the bonds that hold us, crafted relationships that fuel the energy and purpose of our lives. Do we have other friends? Yes, many. This chapter would be a book in itself if I listed all the women I have counted as friends in my life. Their names and faces have come to mind many times as I have worked on this book. But as Ellen Goodman says, "Scattered [throughout my journal] are the words, 'Pat said,' or 'Pat thought.'" These are the imprints of her friend's presence in her life. The clues of deep friendship are not necessarily activities, but thoughts—the influence we have on each other's way of looking at life and living it. This is the kind of friendship I have endeavored to describe.

"Two may talk together under the same roof for many years, yet never really meet," wrote Mary Catherwood, "and two others at first speech are old friends." There is no explanation for why two women fall into step with each other, but there are reasons why we stay together for the long haul. We work at it, for one. We value it enough to keep it going. We get over things, and we go through things. We agree to walk together.

Some of us voice this agreement in faithful actions. We may never say out loud, "I am going to be your Christlike friend," but we say it nonetheless. We live our way into it.

And some of us make a formal agreement, as Mary White and her husband Jerry did with three other couples who were longtime friends: "Our husbands [had] headed to the mountains for a weekend of 'guy' time. As they talked and prayed, they felt God leading us to formalize a covenant of friendship with one another. They returned to talk about this revelation with the wives, who enthusiastically embraced the idea. Together, the eight of us wrote a vision statement for our group: *We will help each other love Jesus for a lifetime.*"

"The Scriptures speak of three kinds of table fellowship that Jesus keeps with his own," wrote Dietrich Bonhoeffer, "daily fellowship at table, the table fellowship of the Lord's Supper, and the final table fellowship in the Kingdom of God. But in all three the one thing that counts is that 'their eyes were opened, and they knew him.'"

This is the reason we are given the Jesus-gift of *friend.* Together He drew us to His side and called us friends. In each other, He reveals Himself and refines His characteristics in us. On the Last Day, we will stand together side by side with the great congregation of all those who are called the friends of Christ. And if we are faithful in this life, you will say of me and I will say of you, "I knew

Him better because I walked with her."

May we all have such a friend as we travel together on the journey of faith.

> *All the nations may walk in the name of their gods; we will walk in the name of the* Lord *our God for ever and ever.*
> —Micah 4:5

Also by Karla Worley

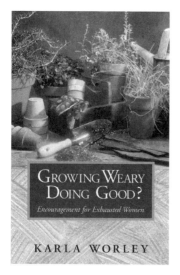

GROWING WEARY
DOING GOOD?
1-56309-438-X

WHEN THE GLASS SLIPPER
DOESN'T FIT
(cowritten with Claire Cloninger)
1-56309-437-1

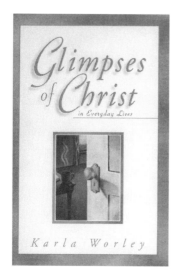

GLIMPSES OF CHRIST
IN EVERYDAY LIVES
1-56309-253-0

AVAILABLE
IN BOOKSTORES
EVERYWHERE.

New Hope
Publishers

Equipping You to Share the Hope of Christ